SINGERS OF ISRAEL
THE BOOK OF PSALMS

BIBLE GUIDES

The twenty-two volumes

★ already published

BIBLE GUIDES

General Editors: William Barclay and F. F. Bruce

No. 10

SINGERS OF ISRAEL

THE BOOK OF PSALMS

by
GEORGE S. GUNN

*Late minister of Broughton Place Church,
Edinburgh*

with a Note on "The Pattern of the Poetry"
by Professor F. F. Bruce
(General Editor, *Bible Guides*)

Published jointly by

LUTTERWORTH PRESS
LONDON

ABINGDON PRESS
NEW YORK AND NASHVILLE

First published 1963

The Biblical quotations in this book are from
the Revised Standard Version of the Bible

*Printed in Great Britain by
Cox & Wyman, Ltd., London, Fakenham and Reading*

To

VIOLET and MARY

in gratitude

CONTENTS

GENERAL INTRODUCTION

THE AIM of Bible Guides is to present in 22 volumes a total view of the Bible, and to present the purpose, plan and power of the Scriptures.

Bible Guides are free from the technicalities of Biblical scholarship but are soundly based on all the generally accepted conclusions of modern Bible reaserch.

They are written in clear, simple, straightforward English. Each author has worked to a comprehensive editorial pattern so that the 22 volumes form a concise conspectus of the Bible.

THE AIM

The aim of Bible Guides is to offer a "guide" to the main themes of each book (or group of books) rather than a commentary on the text of the book. Through Bible Guides the Bible itself will speak its message, reveal its power and declare its purpose.

Bible Guides is essentially an undertaking for non-theologically equipped readers who want to know what the Bible is about, how its various parts came to be written and what their meaning is to-day. But the preacher, teacher, educator and expositor of all ranges of the Christian Church will find Bible Guides a series of books to buy and study. They combine the modern knowledge of the Bible together with all the evangelical zeal of sound Biblical expression—and all done in a handy readable compass.

EDITORIAL PLAN

In our suggestions to the writers of the various books we were careful to make the distinction between a "commentary" and a "guide". Our experience is that an adequate commentary on a book of the Bible requires adequate space and on the part of the student some equipment in the scholarly lore and technicalities of Biblical research. A "guide", however, can be both selective and compressed and do what it sets out to do—guide the reader in an understanding of the book. That has been, and is, our aim.

As general editors we have had a good deal of experience among the various schools of Biblical interpretation. We are constantly surprised at the amount of common Biblical understanding which is acceptable to all types of Christian tradition and churchmanship. We hope that our Bible Guides reflect this and that they will be widely used, and welcomed as a contribution to Biblical knowledge and interpretation in the twentieth century.

THE WRITERS

The writers of Bible Guides represent a widely selected area of Biblical scholars, and all of them have co-operated enthusiastically in the editorial plan. They conceive their work to be that of examination, explanation and exposition of the book(s) of the Bible each is writing about. While they have worked loyally to the pattern we suggested they have been completely free in their presentation. Above all, they have remembered the present power and appeal of the Bible, and have tried to present its message and its authority for life to-day. In this sense Bible Guides is, we think, a fresh venture in the popular understanding of the Scriptures, combined as it is with the scholarly skill of our company of writers. We owe our thanks also to our publishers and their editors, Dr. Emory Stevens Bucke of the Abingdon Press of New York and Nashville, and Dr. Cecil Northcott of the Lutterworth Press of London. Their careful management and attention to publishing detail have given these Bible Guides a world wide constituency.

WILLIAM BARCLAY

F. F. BRUCE

AUTHOR'S FOREWORD

IN A BOOK published a few years ago, *God in the Psalms*, I attempted to examine the larger theological problems raised by the Book of Psalms. These questions are referred to in this book only in the briefest possible way.

The series in which this book is included has a very definite aim. In conformity with this aim, I have endeavoured to give a simple, straightforward guide to the religious ideas of the Book of Psalms as a whole. This, it has to be confessed, is far from easy, because the available material in the Psalms is so varied and comprehensive.

The tendency to make many quotations from the Psalms has had to be kept within bounds. But in addition to the actual quotations which have been judged essential, there are many more references provided. The book will, it is hoped, be a sufficient and reliable guide for those who are not likely to consult all these references; but it will be a richer guide for those who will look them up with care.

Once again I acknowledge my debt to Miss Mabel Isdale for her willing, prompt and competent typing of the manuscript.

GEORGE S. GUNN

THE PSALTER—ITS PURPOSE

THE PSALMS are the heart of the Bible. Many have said so all down the centuries and still more have gladly acknowledged how aptly that description expresses their own feelings. Yet it is subject to one obvious, all-important modification. The part of the Bible which, for Christians, gives full meaning to all the other parts and sends vitality through the entire body of the Scriptures is that which contains the life, teaching, death and resurrection of our Lord. The Psalms are indeed the heart of the Old Testament, the part of the Old Testament which has most deeply and permanently enriched the soul of men.

The Bible as a whole is the Word of God for a twofold reason. In it as nowhere else God conveys to sinful men His offer of mercy and release, revealing Himself as a God who in His Son has taken upon Himself the whole burden of human sin, sorrow and suffering. This, however, is never separated from God's clear call to man to respond to and close with His offer by faith, penitence and obedience. These two—merciful approach and absolute demand—hold the Bible together in vital unity, as with a clasp of gold.

Now it is in worship that man is most likely to receive and understand God's offer, and to be supplied with the inspiration and driving-power to fulfil His demand. For the purposes of worship, both private and public, especially in its latter aspect of human response, there is no book in the Bible which is so valuable. For this very purpose the collection of Psalms was designed, no doubt with great care and judgment. It has so nourished worship in the two highest religions of the world, Jewish and Christian, that it is not now possible to conceive of worship in either of them without the Psalms. All great literatures have produced religious poetry, and it has certain similar features everywhere. Hebrew poetry has its own distinctive marks, and much helpful study has been given to its characteristic forms. But the supreme distinction of the Psalms is that they are so consciously God-centred. All poetry with a religious bent has its intimations and suggestions of God, but the Psalms are far beyond this. They offer us direct contact with God as we read, chant and sing them; and they do it the more forcefully because of their immense variety of form, mood, situation and emotion.

Headway in Devotion

Hosts of nameless people could supply grateful testimony to this fact, but a few conspicuous examples may be given of how people make "headway in devotion" by use of the Psalms. One of Scotland's treasures is the Bible which Mary Slessor used for many years in her gallant pioneering as a missionary in Calabar, Nigeria. There is hardly a tiny corner of marginal space in which she had not written her comments, often penetrating and even pungent. But the Book of Psalms has scarcely a mark. The reason probably is that she used the Scottish Metrical Psalms most of which she likely knew by heart. The total influence of the Psalms upon her may well be reflected in one of the very few passages underlined—some of the closing verses of Psalm

14

104—"May the glory of the Lord endure forever, may the Lord rejoice in His works. I will sing to the Lord as long as I live; I will sing praise to my God while I have being. May my meditation be pleasing to him, for I rejoice in the Lord". In such a prayer is the key to a life of consecration and service.

James Gilmour of Mongolia, another intrepid missionary, says, "When I find I cannot make headway in devotion, I open the Bible at the Psalms and push in my canoe, and let myself be carried along in the stream of devotion which flows through the whole book; the current always sets towards God and in most places is strong and deep".

"The Psalms exhibit the mind of the saints and the hidden treasure of their hearts, the working of their thoughts and their most secret feelings", says Martin Luther. His great co-reformer, John Calvin, puts it thus, "This book I am wont to call an anatomy of all the parts of the soul, for no one will find in himself a single feeling of which the image is not reflected in this mirror". Chrysostom, the golden-mouthed preacher, describes the supreme influence of the Psalms on Christians thus, "When others are asleep, David alone is active". "How is my love for God kindled by the Psalms", exclaims Augustine, and his chief spiritual guide, Ambrose, makes the judgment, "though all Divine Scripture doth breathe the Grace of God, sweet beyond all others is the Book of Psalms".

Timeless and Universal

It is almost certain that never an hour passes now in which the Lord's Prayer is not used somewhere; and many of the Psalms are not far behind. People who are otherwise much divided, in theological standpoint, in type of worship, in depth of experience, are found to be at one in at least a selection of dear, favourite Psalms. Whenever they turn themselves to an approach to God in response to the approach He has already made to them—and that is the essence of worship—the language of a Psalm is found on their lips. Without worship, there could be no survival either for the individual Christian or the Church.

Worship is "worth-ship", for it is the recognition of worth calling out from us the utmost devotion and reverence. That is its evident meaning in such a common expression as "simply worshipping" somebody else; and that is only a faint reflection of the attitude and experience of the true worshipper of God. To be sure, we are never able to see and grasp fully the entire "worth-ship" of God—but we are able to recognize that a supreme, absolute worth belongs to God. In all acts of worship, we strive to fulfil certain aims—to declare openly our adoration and thanksgiving, to keep our need and sin ever before us in confession so that our need may be met and our sin pardoned, to nourish our personal faith amid all the problems, fears, doubts and reverses of life, to make an open witness to others and especially to the rising generation, and to crown and complete our worship by service, gift and sacrifice. It would be a very revealing and satisfying experience to go through the Psalms, or even a section of them, and discover how universal in them are these five notes of worship which have just been mentioned.

Many attempts have been made to assign a Psalm to a particular historical situation, but this does not carry us very far. There have been some brilliant guesses, and a wide and sometimes bewildering diversity of view on this matter exists. But it is not a question of first importance. All discussion of precise date and authorship, while forming an interesting or even valuable introduction to the thought and message of a Psalm, is bound to be inconclusive and to have a broad margin of uncertainty. It is the Psalm itself that is the treasure, not the period or the circumstances in which it was written. What is of supreme value are the timeless and universal truths embodied in the Psalms. If, for example, a Psalm which used confidently to be regarded as having been written by King David or in his time turns out as a result of fuller research to be much later in composition, there is no great loss. The Psalm is still there. It is a case, not of one great Psalm less, but of one great psalmist more—which is sheer gain. But all reliable conclusions on questions of date, circumstances and authorship are to be welcomed for the light they shed on the substantial ideas of the Psalm.

There is probably no book of the Old Testament upon which the views of scholars have changed more than the Psalter, as a result of the very large and very able work done by scholars in the last generation. The three greatest names in this field are Gunkel, Mowinckel and Pedersen. It can be safely said that the tendency has been to put many of the Psalms to an earlier period in Israel's history. Some parts of the Psalter, e.g. the first Davidic section (Psalms 1-41) may well have been collected soon after the Ezra and Nehemiah period. In time, maybe a century or more afterwards, a second Davidic collection would be added (Psalms 51-72); and still later other more varied groups of Psalms. The actual timing of the composition of the Psalms cannot be determined with any certainty; but it can be claimed that the period covered by the entire collection is very long, from the early monarchy to the end of the Persian empire. It is not to be questioned that some Psalms go back to David and earlier, and it is probable that some are as late as the Maccabean struggle. That means about a thousand years—a period somewhat similar to that which is covered by the Old Testament writings as a whole.

Hymnbook of the Temple

The Psalms are individual in character and, when actually written, may not have had public worship in view. It is most unlikely that they were written specifically for such a purpose. The reason why they were subsequently collected for that purpose was that their quality was so suitable for it. In most of the Psalms, the religious conceptions are developed conceptions, removed far from the primitive and elementary in the ideas of God's nature, purposes and rule held by their writers. Whenever their writers lived, they were men who in their own thought and conviction had come thus far. This fact largely determined the selection of the Psalms, doubtless from many sources and earlier collections. The Book of Psalms is "a collection of collections", but the original unity of the original collections has probably been broken up and the selected Psalms distributed over the larger, final collection. What is of supreme importance is that it was for the purposes of worship that the collection was made, in very much the same way as for the same purpose a modern hymnbook is constructed.

This is the measure of truth in the now general description of the Psalter as "the hymnbook of the Second Temple". The first Temple was erected in Solomon's reign, probably about 950 B.C., and it was destroyed when the state of Judah fell in 586 B.C. A second Temple, sometimes called Zerubbabel's, was dedicated about 516 B.C. and it suffered great spoliation and destruction both in 54 B.C. and 37 B.C. In this second Temple much that had been the spiritual glory of Solomon's Temple had disappeared—the Ark of the Covenant was burnt when Jerusalem fell, and so too the tables of the law, Aaron's rod and the golden shields. After the exile, the office of King was not restored; and so the Second Temple was more of a priestly sanctuary than a royal chapel.

When the disastrous calamity of the exile was over and those who returned from exile gave themselves to the heavy and often disheartening task of rebuilding the life of a fallen nation, they gave their first attention to a rebuilding of the people's worship. The instinct here was very sound—that it has to be around its religion and worship, and by the power and purpose supplied by religion that any hopeful or lasting reconstruction must proceed. This is the supreme emphasis of Ezekiel, who lived through these dark days. So the leaders of the restored community gave first place to a restoration of worship—with acts of dedication, public vows, fast days, festivals connected with Harvest, Atonement and Tabernacles, and above all the observance of Sabbath. As time passed, suitable Psalms became associated with these great occasions; and the connection would get closer and closer as the generations passed. The great acts and occasions of worship were not created by these leaders after the exile, for they had been a part of the fabric of Israel's worship almost from the beginning. But it was the community after the exile that collected and arranged the Psalter; and it must have been believed that in the great thoughts of the Psalms, recited or sung, there was a strong safeguard against the too easy tendency of ritual acts to degenerate into empty formality.

On this whole issue of the connection of the Psalms with worship, it is important to ask what kind of men they were, and what principles of worship they held, who were responsible for this connection. In modern study of the Psalms, a good deal of attention is given to a figure of whom we heard little before—the cult-prophet. The Psalms are obviously saturated with the teaching of the great prophets, but the great prophets may not have been as interested in the outward forms of worship as people in the priestly tradition are. The distinction, however, between prophet and priest has often been too sharply drawn. There have always been men who held a middle position between prophet and priest, loyal to the best insights of the prophets in religious and moral matters and yet very careful about the forms of worship of the people. It is that kind of man who is now described as "the cult-prophet", and it seems certain that they are mainly responsible for the splendid, far-reaching and momentous work of compiling the Psalms. Like people who believe that it is right and wise to have a foot in both camps, they may not have been popular and would often be misunderstood. Prophets and priests can both be faithful, each in his own way. The cult-prophets after the exile prevented a rejection of the prophetic teaching when they selected Psalms for worship which are so full of that teaching; and that also was the best way to keep at bay the mere sacerdotalist, concerned to magnify the power of the priesthood, whose influence creeps in all too easily. There is an old saying "Quench the prophet, you kindle the priest". It contains a salutary warning for the Church of every age; but, when it is held to mean that prophet and priest can have no use for each other, it is extremely false. The very existence of the Psalter proves that.

David—and the Psalms

It is a long, strong tradition to speak of "the Psalms of David". The claim of all the Psalms for David cannot be upheld, but that does not mean that the tradition is unfounded. By the time that the story of David's reign was written down, he was already known as "the sweet singer of Israel" (2 Samuel 23 : 1). In his career also there were not a few decisive incidents which are very similar to the situations described in some of the Psalms. In particular, he seems to have been just the kind of man to write sacred songs, to inspire others to do so and to exalt a nation's worship. The whole question of the association of David's name with the Psalter is best understood in relation to the importance which he attached to the centrality of worship.

David's reign was in many ways the most brilliant reign in human history, and there is nothing more significant in it than what is described in 2 Samuel 6—the decision to bring up the Ark of God into Jerusalem, which he had made the political capital of the country. Thus he started a process which has continued to the present day, by which Jerusalem was given a place in the religious life of the world which is unique. Such it is for the two highest religions of mankind which hold it as a peculiarly sacred spot. To make Jerusalem both the political and the religious capital was the master-stroke of a man of strong conviction and deep experience. It was indeed David's way of saying "Unless the Lord builds the house, those who build it labour in vain. Unless the Lord watches over the city, the watchman stays awake in vain" (Psalm 127: 1). He began by providing a simple shelter for the Ark, and he had it in mind to build a worthy Temple for it and prepared for that all his life (1 Chronicles 29). By this emphatic insistence on the union of religious and civic life, David showed himself to be the man after God's own heart.

A surprisingly large place is given to the Ark and its varying fortunes in the Old Testament. It is mentioned about two hundred times in the Old Testament, by at least twenty-two different names. Its loss was reckoned the greatest calamity that the country could endure. When Solomon built the Temple, the Ark was given a special place in the inner sanctuary, the Holy of Holies, where it remained for over four hundred years. In the later temples there was no Ark.

All the significant associations of the Ark are with worship. It reminds men that the supreme reverence of life is in the presence of God Who is always near. To David, at his best, religion was the crowning reality of life, not the phantasy of a dream world. The Sovereign God is on His throne. He has never abdicated and never will. "The Lord reigns, let the earth rejoice; the Lord reigns, let the peoples tremble" (Psalms 97: 1; 99: 1). "Lift up your heads, O gates! and be lifted up, O ancient doors! that the King of glory may come in" (Psalm 24: 7).

The Ark was often called "the Ark of the Covenant" and among its contents were the tables of the Covenant, according to Hebrews 9: 4–5. It is said in Kings 8: 9 that, when Solomon dedicated the Temple, "there was nothing in the ark except the two tables of stone which Moses put there at Horeb, where the Lord made a covenant with the people of Israel". In this way the Ark reminded the people that God requires obedience, and that acceptable religion and worship imply unquestioning obedience to a God who has every right to command.

The supreme joy of life also lies in worship. The bringing of the Ark into Jerusalem was made an occasion of great joy, with the shouting and dancing associated with victory and triumph. David believed in "serving the Lord with gladness" and in "making a joyful noise to the rock of our salvation"(Psalm 95: 1). We are told in 1 Chronicles 15: 27, how David was accompanied by the singers; and in 1 Chronicles 16 we read how he appointed two songs to be sung at the dedication of the Ark, with a doxology ("O give thanks to the Lord!") at the close (1 Chronicles 16: 34), now found in Psalm 106: 1 and 48. The source of all religious joy is the knowledge of what God has done for us, that He honours us by calling us to be His fellow-workers, and that we now are able to serve and witness with the comfort and inspiration of a long tradition behind us. That tradition of worship has been infinitely expanded and matured by the use of the Psalms. No wonder that David's name should be specially linked with the Psalms, since his insights into worship are so clear and sound.

The Bible in Miniature

"You may rightly call the Psalter a Bible in miniature," said Martin Luther. That means that it holds a special relationship to the Old Testament and the New. It is the great gathering-up book of the Old Testament, for in it the whole essence of thought and religion found in the entire range of the Old Testament is distilled. The problem which is dealt with so dramatically in Job is treated profoundly in Psalm 73. The decisive events of the Exodus are gathered up vividly in Psalms 105 and 106. The story of Creation has its poetical counterpart in Psalm 104. There is not one great thought in the prophets without its parallel in the Psalms. To this we have to add that, whereas in the books of history and prophecy God is speaking to men in the events and in the preaching, in the Psalms man's words are addressed to God. They contain what select souls were experiencing in the changing moods of thanksgiving, repentance, questioning, resolve; and this is the reason for the universal use of the Psalms.

It is a common thing to bind in one book the Psalms and the New Testament. This signifies that, if only one book of the Old Testament is to be chosen to set beside the whole New Testament, it can only be the Psalms. In the early Christian centuries, candidates for the ministry were required to know the Psalms by heart along with large portions of the New Testament. When the missionary-translator undertakes the task of giving the Bible to people in their own tongue, he usually starts with the Gospels and follows them with the Psalms.

There are, it is reckoned, two hundred and eighty-seven verses of the Old Testament quoted in the New, and of these one hundred and sixteen are from the Psalms. In the writings of Paul and in the Epistle to the Hebrews we find the Psalms used to support the argument being set forth. In Romans 3 Paul quotes from Psalms 51: 4; 14: 1–2; 5: 9; 140: 3; 10: 7; 36: 1; and in chapter 15: 9 and 11 he refers to Psalms 18: 49; 117: 1. The author of Hebrews makes a great use of the Psalms in chapter 1—Psalms 2: 7; 45: 6–7; 102: 25–27; 110: 1; and, in chapter 5, Psalm 110: 4; in chapter 10, Psalm 40: 6–8; and finally Psalm 118: 6 in chapter 13: 6.

Although our Lord probably had no Bible of His own, He too turns to the Psalms. With the other pilgrims to Jerusalem He would sing, as a boy of twelve, the Songs of Ascent.

Our Lord uses words from Psalms to describe His own Person—Matthew 21: 16 where He quotes Psalm 8: 2; Matthew 21: 42 where He quotes Psalm 118: 22–23; Matthew 22: 43–44 where He quotes Psalm 110: 1.

In the Upper Room at the Last Supper, He would with His disciples sing the "Hallel" (Psalms 113–118) (Matthew 26: 30). On the Cross, He meditates on the Psalms—"My God, My God, why hast thou forsaken me" (22:1) and "Into thy hand I commit my spirit" (31:5). The Risen Christ tells His disciples that the Law, the prophets and the Psalms speak of Him (Luke 24: 44-45). In the worship of the Christian Church at Corinth, the Psalms were employed (1 Corinthians 14:26); and they have never ceased to find their fitting place in the whole Church till now. So much is this so that it can be claimed that "a history of the use of the Psalter would be a history of the spiritual life of the Church".

2

THE PSALTER—ITS PLAN

THERE IS probably no book in the Bible the structure of which is more difficult to describe. It may be taken for granted that the 150 Psalms are a small selection of a much larger number in existence, and that for good reasons they represent "a survival of the fittest". There is no known reason why the final selection should have been 150, not more and not less. What is certain is that the principle of comprehensiveness has been applied to a marvellous degree. Other Old Testament books have poetical sections, but this book only is entirely poetical. In view of their immense variety of theme and form, it is hard to see how some people maintain that they are not attracted to the Psalms because they are so much alike. It is more understandable that some find the Psalms a very difficult book to study because of their extensive variety. With such a range of themes, how can this "Hebrew Golden Treasury" be classified?

It is not apparent that there has been any definite principle or plan in the order of the Psalms. Two Psalms with the same emphasis of thought do not usually lie next each other, but may be widely separated. Yet even a first careful reading will show that some kind of plan emerges. Psalms which are closely related in thought are occasionally found together, e.g. 3 and 4, 9 and 10, 42 and 43, 105 and 106. This is still more marked in 93–100 where the great common theme is the kingly majesty of God, and in 145–150 with their resonant call to worshippers to praise the Lord. Also, there are groups of Psalms which have an identical inscription attached to them, e.g. 56–60, or the Songs of Ascent, 120–134, which were most commonly used on pilgrimage to the local shrine or, oftener, up to the Temple.

Then there are Psalms which appear twice in whole or part—14 is repeated in 53; 40: 13–17 in 70; 57: 7–11 and 60: 5–12 in 108; Psalm 31: 3 appears again in 71: 1–3. This may be explained by the fact that several earlier collections were being drawn on. But it may well be significant that the Psalm which is repeated in full, with only the smallest change, is the one which exposes the folly of man living as if there was no God. Then there are Psalms in the acrostic form—34, 37, 111–112, and 119—in which the acrostic use of the letters of the Hebrew alphabet is variously employed.

The opening and the closing Psalms of the collection must have been carefully and deliberately chosen. Psalm 1 stands as a most appropriate introduction to the Psalter, with its sustained contrast of the two ways of life, the godly and the ungodly. Not only does this contrast often appear in other Psalms, but the very purpose of that worship for the sake of which the Psalter was compiled is to lead men to serve and glorify God in choosing the godly way and rejecting the ungodly. Psalm 150 in its own way is an equally suitable close for the Psalter. Under the strong compulsion of the great thoughts of God unfolded throughout the Psalms, the only appropriate final call is "Let everything that breathes praise the Lord. Praise the Lord". These two Psalms are as fitting an introduction and conclusion to the Psalter as Genesis and Revelation are to the Bible as a whole.

The Five Books

There is now a long tradition behind the division of the Psalter into five books—and this goes back to a time before the Psalter was translated into the Greek version of the Septuagint. The five books are 1–41, 42–72, 73–89, 90–106, 107–150. The most probable reason for this division is to secure correspondence with the five books of Moses, the Pentateuch, which stand at the opening of the Bible, thus making the Psalter a kind of "second Pentateuch", associated with David's name. At the end of these five books is a doxology—41: 13; 72: 18–19; 89: 52; 106: 48; 150.

The actual title of this book in Hebrew is *Tehillim* which means "hymn of praise". Obviously all the Psalms are not strictly of that character, and in fact only one psalm, 145, is called a *tehillah*. The other great Hebrew word of worship is *tephilloth*, prayers; and again only one psalm, 17, is called a *tephillah*. The most common Hebrew title is *mizmor*, which lies behind the Greek title *psalmos* from which we get our English term "psalm". As many as 57 of the Psalms have this Hebrew title, and it is generally regarded as having to do with the string instruments that accompanied their use. It is noteworthy that the New Testament usually refers to this book as "The book of Psalms"— Luke 20: 42; Acts 1: 20.

Some of the titles of the Psalms refer to authorship. In all, 73 Psalms are ascribed to David—all in Book 1 with the exception of 1, 2, 10, 33; 51–65 and 68–70 in Book 2; 86, the only one so ascribed in Book 3; 101 and 103 in Book 4; and 107–110, 122, 124, 131, 133, 138–145, in Book 5. At the close of Psalm 72 we find the note, "the prayers of David, the son of Jesse, are ended". But the title of Psalm 72 ascribes it to Solomon. One Psalm, 90, a prayer, is ascribed to Moses. The words do not mean that there are no more Davidic Psalms after 72, any more than the similar words in Job 31: 40, "the words of Job are ended", mean that Job's voice is not to be heard again in the book. Job's main dialogue with his three friends is completed; and similarly the main bulk of Davidic Psalms are to be found in the two collections that make up Books 1 and 2. There is a group of Psalms which are said to be connected with special incidents in David's life—these are 3, 7, 18, 34, 51, 52, 54, 56, 57, 59, 60, 63, 142. All this shows that the source connected with David provided the largest basic portion of the Psalter. In the New Testament, the association of certain Psalms with David is evident in Matthew 22: 43; Mark 12: 36; Luke 20: 42-44; Acts 1: 16-20; 2: 25-28; 4: 25; Romans 4: 6-8; 11: 9-10; Hebrews 4: 7.

A second distinct group of twelve is the "Asaph" group—50, 73-83; and a third group of eleven is the "Korah" group; 42-49, 84, 85, 87, 88. These are held to be guilds of temple singers who had been given special responsibility for leading the worship. The "Songs of Ascent" are fifteen in number, 120-134, and the Hallelujah Psalms are also fifteen, 104-106, 111-113, 115-117, 135, 146-150. It is unnecessary to discuss to what extent all these titles are original, and it is not a matter of primary importance.

There is a group of 34 Psalms which are sometimes referred to as "orphan Psalms", because they have no title either of authorship or musical instruction—1, 2, 10, 33, 71, and a large number in the section 90-150.

There are titles of another kind attached to many of the Psalms—and these have to do with musical directions or explanations as to the use of the psalm. We have seen that the title *mizmor* is attached to 57 Psalms with reference to stringed instruments. The term *shir*, meaning "song" is found with 30 Psalms. *Maschil* is the title of 13 Psalms, all of a deep, reflective type.

29

Michtam describes 6 Psalms, and this very obscure title may have something to do with the idea of atonement for sin.

Such titles as "For the Chief Musician" or "to the Choir-master" as it might now be put; "with stringed instruments" (*neginoth*); "with wind instruments" or "for the flutes" (Psalm 5); "according to the Gittith" (Psalms 8, 81, 84), probably referring to the harp; "according to Jeduthun" (Psalms 39, 62, 77), probably referring to a melody called after David's chief musician, all reflect considerations of the time and the music. Some titles refer to special occasions for the use of the Psalm—92 for the Sabbath Day, 38 and 70 for Memorial occasions, 30 for the dedication of the House of God. It is not possible to attain certainty as to the meaning of some of the titles, for some are late and unreliable. Many of the Psalms, however, have no such directions. There is, however, abundance of evidence for the use of music in Old Testament worship—flutes, trumpets, organs, harps, lutes and cymbals.

The curious term "Selah" is used 71 times in 39 Psalms and three times in Habakkuk 3: 3, 9, 13. It has been held to be a divider of stanzas, an emphatic Amen, a sign for a pause or for a repetition or for a crescendo. If its origin is in the Hebrew word *salal*, its meaning would be likely to be a call to worshippers to raise their voice up in a united ascription of glory to God, a full doxology for voices and instruments together.

A Structural Plan

One of the most fascinating attempts to interpret the structural plan of the Psalter has been made by Hermann Gunkel in his classification of the Psalms according to type and theme. Such a division as he makes is almost certainly too rigid and there is bound to be much overlapping. But it is given here for the very practical reason that a re-reading of the Psalms with this classification in view will often be helpful and illuminating.

The division of Gunkel is as follows:

1. *The Hymn* for normal worship—Psalms 8, 19, 29, 33, 47, 65, 68, 93, 96, 97, 98, 99, 100, 103, 104, 105, 111, 113, 114, 115, 117, 118, 135, 136, 145, 146, 147, 148, 149, 150.

2. *Communal Laments*, on occasions of calamity and misfortune—Psalms 44, 58, 74, 79, 80, 83, 106, 125.

3. *Royal Psalms*—dealing with the King's sacral significance, i.e. his importance as representing God's relationship to His people, in Israel's life and worship—Psalms 2, 18, 20, 21, 45, 72, 101, 110, 132.

4. *Individual Laments*, full of deep emotion on the part of the personal worshipper—Psalms 3, 5, 6, 7, 13, 17, 22, 25, 26, 27, 28, 31, 35, 38, 39, 42–43, 51, 54, 55, 56, 57, 59, 61, 63, 64, 69, 70, 71, 86, 88, 102, 109, 120, 130, 140, 141, 142, 143.

5. *Individual Songs of Thanksgiving*—not a large class—Psalms 18, 30, 32, 34, 41, 46, 92, 116, 118, 138.

6. *Songs of Pilgrimage*—a small group—Psalms 84, 122.

7. *Communal Songs of Thanksgiving*—also a small group—Psalms 67, 124.

8. *Wisdom Poetry*—closely akin to "Proverbs"—Psalms 1, 37, 49, 73, 112, 127, 128, 133.

9. *Liturgy*—Psalms 2, 15, 24, 110, 132, 134.

The overflow between these sections will be evident as we read the Psalms carefully, and there are points at which the division seems to have no very clear reason. It will be noticed also that some psalms defy such a classification even for Gunkel. Indeed the most helpful plan that can be sought for in the Psalms should rest on the basis of the great conceptions of God and life

which hold the Psalter together as a whole, and which are funda-
mental to all higher religion. It will be something of that kind
which is to be presented in the following pages.

THE PATTERN OF THE POETRY
by F. F. Bruce

The poetry of the Psalms, like Old Testament poetry in
general, is characterized by certain rhythmical patterns which are
to a considerable extent preserved in translation. So far as
rhythm of sound is concerned, this is mainly a question of a regular pattern of stressed syllables. More important, however, is
rhythm of sense, which in Old Testament poetry takes the form
of "parallelism". That is to say, what is essentially the same
idea is expressed twice over in two parallel clauses; the idea is the
same, but the words are different.

It is simplest to explain the various forms of parallelism by
actual examples. There are three main forms: complete parallelism, incomplete parallelism, and step-parallelism.

Complete Parallelism. Here we have two lines where each
significant word in the one corresponds to a significant word in
the other. The parallelism may be *synonymous* (the same thought),
thus:

> The Lord of hosts is with us;
> the God of Jacob is our refuge (Psalm 46: 7, 11).

Or it may be *antithetic* (a contrast), thus:

> They will collapse and fall;
> but we shall rise and stand upright (Psalm 20: 8).

32

Or it may be *emblematic* (a comparison), where the situation in one line is compared to the situation in the adjoining line, thus:

> As a father pities his children,
> so the Lord pities those who fear him (Psalm 103 : 13).

Sometimes the parallelism is more elaborate, and consists in the balancing of groups of lines rather than of single lines. A good example is provided by Psalm 27: 1:

> The Lord is my light and my salvation;
>   whom shall I fear?
> The Lord is the stronghold of my life;
>   of whom shall I be afraid?

This rhythm, in which lines of three and two stressed syllables alternate, is often called the "dirge" rhythm, because it is the characteristic rhythm of the book of Lamentations, but Psalm 27: 1 shows that it can also serve as the vehicle of joyful praise.

Incomplete Parallelism. Sometimes one word in a line has no counterpart in the neighbouring line. Consider, for example, Psalm 40: 2:

> He drew me up from the desolate pit,
>   out of the miry bog.

Here there is no verb in the second line; it is understood from the first line. The result is once again an alternation of three and two stressed syllables. Sometimes an additional stressed syllable will be provided in the second line to preserve the same number as in

B   33

the first line, but not so here: here we have what is called incomplete parallelism *without compensation*. For an example of incomplete parallelism *with compensation* take Psalm 1 : 5 :

> Therefore the wicked will not stand in the judg-
> > ment,
> nor sinners in the congregation of the righteous.

Here, as in Psalm 40 : 2, the verb is omitted in the second line, but here the number of stressed syllables is made up by using a heavier phrase, "the congregation of the righteous", in the second line as the counterpart of "the judgment" in the preceding lines. Sometimes there is still less parallelism of meaning and correspondingly more compensation in the provision of stressed syllables, until the point is reached where we have all compensation and no real parallelism (the construction sometimes called *formal parallelism*), as in Psalm 27 : 6 :

> And now my head shall be lifted up
> above my enemies round about me.

Here we have three stressed syllables in each line, but no single word in the one line has a counterpart in meaning in the other.

Step-parallelism. Occasionally part of one line is repeated in the next, and made the starting-point for a fresh step; this process may be repeated from the second to the third line. A good example of this is found in Psalm 29 : 1 :

> Ascribe to the Lord, O heavenly beings,
> ascribe to the Lord glory and strength.
> Ascribe to the Lord the glory of his name;
> worship the Lord in holy array.

34

Here the step-parallelism is illustrated by the first three lines; lines 3 and 4 stand in complete synonymous parallelism the one to the other. Another example comes in Psalm 92:9:

> For, lo, thy enemies, O Lord,
>> for, lo, thy enemies shall perish;
>> all evildoers shall be scattered.

Here again lines 1 and 2 illustrate step-parallelism; lines 2 and 3 illustrate complete synonymous parallelism.

The recognition of these patterns will add considerably to our appreciation of the beauty of the Psalter.

Strophic Arrangement. Some of the Psalms are divided into strophes. One sign of a strophic arrangement is the recurrence of a refrain. The recurring refrain in Psalms 42 and 43 (originally a single psalm) marks the end of three strophes, at verses 5 and 11 of Psalm 42 and verse 5 of Psalm 43. A similar strophic arrangement is indicated in Psalm 46 by the refrain "The LORD of hosts is with us; the God of Jacob is our refuge" (verses 7 and 11); but verses 1–7 probably formed two strophes, their dividing point being still marked by the "Selah" at the end of verse 3 which may suggest that the refrain was originally sung here too. Psalm 80 is divided into four strophes by the refrain "Restore us, O God . . ." (or "Turn again, O God . . .") in verses 3, 7, 14, 19. The second part of Psalm 24 shows a more involved strophic pattern, with the repeated command "Lift up your heads, O gates!" and the question and response "Who is the King of glory?" Strophic arrangement is also involved in the acrostic schemes found in some of the Psalms. The most outstanding instance of an acrostic in the Psalter is Psalm 119, whose twenty-two sections are formal strophes, corresponding to the twenty-two letters of the Hebrew alphabet, arranged so that the eight sentences in the first section each begin with the first letter, the eight sentences in the second section with the second letter, and so on to the eight sentences of the last section, which each begin with the twenty-second letter.

3

THE PSALTER—ITS SUBSTANCE

(i) THE GLORY OF GOD

It has been already noted that the Lord's Prayer and the Psalms have a place all their own in the life and worship of devout people. The point at which they are most linked together is their common emphasis that true and acceptable worship begins and ends in adoration of the glory of God and their common understanding that the glory of God means His varied ways of self-manifestation to men.

Doubtless it is true that we can begin our prayers at any point, according to need and mood; and it is obvious enough that the Psalms begin at many different points—it may be exultation or dejection, it may be confidence or despair, it may be thanksgiving or perplexity. If the Lord's Prayer is to be taken as a model prayer, it is significant that the note on which it begins and ends is adoration—"Hallowed be thy Name: for thine is the Kingdom, the power and the glory forever." Prayer and praise do not rise very high except we have in our mind the commanding thought of the majesty and magnificence of God. Behind the Lord's Prayer is an older Jewish prayer—"May His great name be magnified and hallowed in the world which He has created"— and there we have an idea of which there are many resounding echoes in the Psalms.

If this note of adoration is lacking, we are neglecting the plain example of Jesus and of the Psalms. Our Lord would not have us to rush on to prayers for the coming of the Kingdom, or for daily bread, or for forgiveness, or for deliverance from temptation, till we have first prayed for reverence to God's Name as revealed by Him. In that way we grasp the very truth about God and so we are set free from idolatry which is an enthronement of falsehood about God. Unless the God-fearing attitude is present, all the rest is bound to be out of order. Our Lord associated in His Prayer the glory of God and the good of men; if God is given His first place of honour and glory, all the other things will be added to us. The true good of everybody is made secure by giving God His rightful place, for the awestruck recognition of God by man is the mainspring of all action. This is one of the chief lessons of Isaiah's call (Isaiah 6), and it is the ever-recurring refrain of the Psalter as a whole. As the Scottish Shorter Catechism of 1648 puts it in its very first answer, "Man's chief end is to glorify God and to enjoy Him forever."

The Benefits and Blessings of Worship

In Exodus 33 : 18, we find Moses, burdened with his heavy and sometimes thankless task of leadership, pleading with God, "I beseech thee, show me thy glory." He is reminded that it is impossible for man to have such a request fully granted, but there is revealed to him as much of God's glory as he can bear or comprehend. The Psalms in their many references to the glory of God show the same desire, taking for granted that man cannot fulfil his life unless he see the glory of God. His glory fills the whole earth (72: 19). It is declared by the heavens (19: 1) and yet is above the heavens (113: 4; 148: 13). Man's very cry for

38

help is "for the glory of thy Name" (79: 9), and it is the joy of the saints (149: 5). In a world of change and uncertainty, it is the unalterable fact—"the glory of the Lord shall endure forever" (104: 31). The manifold appeal of the Psalms for worship is set also in these terms—and it is addressed both to the heavenly beings and to the dwellers upon the earth—"Ascribe to the Lord, O heavenly beings, ascribe to the Lord glory and strength. Ascribe to the Lord the glory of his name; worship the Lord in holy array" (29: 1–2). "Ascribe to the Lord, O families of the peoples, ascribe to the Lord glory and strength! Ascribe to the Lord the glory due to his name; bring an offering, and come into his courts! Worship the Lord in holy array; tremble before him, all the earth" (96: 7–9). "The heavens proclaim his righteousness, and all the peoples behold his glory" (97: 6).

Psalm 117 is the shortest of the Psalms, and also the shortest chapter in the Bible, and the middle chapter of the 1,189 chapters. It seems peculiarly fitted to occupy this place, for it calls upon all people to praise and extol the Lord, and in very few words gives the reasons why it is so seemly and beneficial to do so—"great is his steadfast love toward us; and the faithfulness of the Lord endures for ever". This is what men see in God when they are lifted up to the central summit of the Old Testament revelation. Or, if we turn one page back to Psalm 115, we find the same thought—"Not to us, O Lord, not to us, but to thy name give glory, for the sake of thy steadfast love and thy faithfulness". Then follows a devastating comparison between the true God and the idols of the nations (115: 3–8; 135: 15–18). Behind these verses there is not only a total statement of the obvious deficiencies of the idols, but also by implication the deeper thought that the Creator of the human ear must be a perfect hearer, and the Creator of the human eye a perfect seer—a thought more expressly stated in 94: 9–11. In Psalm 115, the line of thought proceeds to a call for trust in a God who will bless those that fear Him, both small and great, and for praise continually to a God who is great enough to be maker of heaven and earth and who condescends to give increase to human beings and to bless them and their children. This same combination of activities in God is met again in 147: 2–4, where it is said that it is the same God who counts and names the stars and heals the broken-hearted.

There is a great deal in the Psalter on the benefits and blessings of worship. There are few influences more effective in keeping the soul of man in its proper relationship to God than regular and earnest expression of gratitude—and so the element of thanksgiving is very prominent. "O give thanks to the Lord"(105: 1; 106: 1, 47; 107: 1; 118: 1; 136: 1, 2, 3, 26). "I wash my hands in innocence, and go about thy altar, O Lord, singing aloud a song of thanksgiving, and telling all thy wondrous deeds" (26: 6–7). Whenever we enter His gates, it is to be with thanksgiving (100: 4). The man who has passed through the sore experiences of Psalm 116 resolves to "offer to thee the sacrifice of thanksgiving" (v. 17); and the sense of it should be so strong that even at midnight we should rise to praise God (119: 62). There is, of course, the identical emphasis in all the passages which summon men to praise the Lord. This is the privilege of men while they have life, for some of the psalmists have no assurance that there will be any opportunity to praise God after death (30: 9; 88: 10; 119: 175). A man who is alive and alert to the manifold greatness and goodness of God will want to bring repeated acts of praise, even seven times a day (119: 164). Psalm 50 is one which deserves to be better known and more used than it is, and it finishes with a declaration put on God's own lips: "He who brings thanksgiving as his sacrifice honours me; to him who orders his way aright I

40

will show the salvation of God." It is foolish to suggest, as some do, that this is a sign of empty vainglory attributed to God. A study of the earlier verses of the psalm, especially 7–15, would make that suggestion appear empty.

Outward Forms and the Inward Spirit

A second essential feature of worship is sincerity, and in turn that is quickened and enriched by worship. Old Testament religion has its own set forms of worship, as every religion must; and these were closely connected with the sacrifices which accompanied worship. There are many passages in the prophets and in the psalms which appear to suggest that these writers completely disapproved of sacrifice—Amos 4: 4; 5: 21–25; Hosea 6: 6; 9: 4; 12: 11; Micah 6: 6–8; Jeremiah 6: 20; 7: 10–15, 21–23; Psalm 50: 8–14; 51: 16–17; 40: 6. But the full evidence does not warrant such a drastic conclusion. What these passages are concerned to state is of supreme importance—that the outward forms of worship are worthless and harmful unless there is a sincere inwardness of spirit behind them.

The peril of all external forms of worship is that they tend to take on a value all for themselves, and then they no longer express life. At that point people come to be satisfied just with minimum requirements and performance; and this is an ever-present, deadly danger of every worshipping community. There are passages in the Psalms too where the sacrifices are in no sense belittled—20: 3; 50: 5; 66: 13; 118: 27; 141: 2. Out of his profound experience of penitence, the writer of Psalm 51 declares that, once the clean heart is created in him, once he offers to God the acceptable sacrifice of the broken and contrite heart, then he can offer the right sacrifices, burnt offerings and bulls upon the altar, and in them God will take delight (vv. 10–12, 16–19). Two of the most important psalms, dealing with the inward state and the moral qualifications of true worshippers, are 15 and 24. There are also psalms—notably six: 46, 48, 66, 84, 87, 122— which celebrate the greatness and glory of the earthly shrines where God meets with His people; but it is clear enough that the greatness and glory of these places lies in the reflection within them of the ineffable greatness and glory of the God who has chosen to set His name there. In this sense also we should read the Psalms which may have been specially connected with the Sabbath—especially 92, or with the great festivals—especially 120-134, 47 and 81.

It is not to be expected that people will persevere in worship unless they find in it relief and strength for immediate needs— such as depression, crushing of the spirit through trouble and misfortune, trial of faith occasioned by severe doubt and anxiety; and, with such problems in mind, we turn to Psalms 42, 43, 73 and 107. In worship also man seeks a force which bridges the gulfs of life which separate and isolate him from others; and that blessing is unfolded in Psalms like 20, 21, 46, 66, 68, 87 and 135. From such worship there is an inevitable overflow affecting the lives of those who do not yet believe, and so we have in the Psalms the clear suggestion that worship is a great witness to the world which lives away from God—52: 9; 99: 5–9. Also, as we would expect, the Psalms do not neglect the responsibility which lies upon one generation to transmit to the next generation their faith and the decisive events upon which their faith rests—78, 105 and 106.

Finally, worship is the source of joy in life. When it is so understood and experienced, it will be a joy to offer worship, not a mere duty, or a burden, or a nuisance. This conception appears

42

prominently in Psalms 26: 6-12; 27: 3-6; 42, 43, 65, 84, 92, 100, 118, 122. At its best and highest, Old Testament worship offered to the people something in which they could and did share with exuberant delight. The gathering of the people at the local shrine and at the central Temple was often, as it should ever be, a supreme pleasure and privilege and inspiration. It is beyond imagination that the day will ever come when worshippers will not be moved and thrilled by

> All people that on earth do dwell
> Sing to the Lord with cheerful voice:
> Him serve with mirth, His praise forth tell,
> Come ye before Him and rejoice.

God's Glory in Nature

The first and most obvious sphere of God's glory is in Nature all around us. Some of the best-known, most vivid and most vigorous Psalms deal with this subject. The God of the Psalms is the sovereign Creator and Ruler of heaven and earth, and the earth has been appointed by Him and furnished by Him to be the home of man and beast. "The heavens are the Lord's heavens, but the earth he has given to the sons of men" (115: 16). Here is the clear suggestion that God has fixed the bounds of man's habitation, and it is easy to guess what the writer of these verses would say of modern man's daring incursions far beyond the domains of the earth. Equally clearly, the eternity of the Creator over against His creation is stated in Psalm 102: 25-27—"Of old thou didst lay the foundation of the earth, and the heavens are the work of thy hands. They will perish, but thou dost endure; they will all wear out like a garment. Thou changest them like raiment, and they pass away; but thou art the same, and thy years have no end."

There is no mixing up of God and Nature in the Bible, and so there is nothing like Nature-worship. God and His Creation are distinct, and it is wholly dependent on Him for its origin, its character, and its continuance. Yet man can learn true lessons of God by observing His handiwork—"Thy steadfast love, O Lord, extends to the heavens, thy faithfulness to the clouds. Thy righteousness is like the mountains of God, thy judgments are like the great deep; man and beast thou savest, O Lord" (36: 5–6). "As the mountains are round about Jerusalem, so the Lord is round about his people" (125: 2).

The writers of the Psalms, living in a pre-scientific era, describe a direct, immediate relationship between God and Nature. This emphasis is ultimate truth, whatever modern science may disclose of the processes and methods by which Nature works. "The sea is his, for he made it; for his hands formed the dry land" (95: 5). "For he commanded, and raised the stormy wind, which lifted up the waves of the sea" (107: 25). "He made the storm be still, and the waves of the sea were hushed. He turns rivers into a desert, springs of water into thirsty ground, a fruitful land into a salty waste, because of the wickedness of its inhabitants" (107: 29, 33–35). In Psalm 148, the writer summons the heavens and all their hosts to praise God's Name, "for he commanded and they were created, and he established them forever and ever; he fixed their bounds which cannot be passed" (148: 5–6, cf. Amos 3: 6; Daniel 4: 25). The greatest of all the Nature Psalms is the grandest expression of this conception—104, than which there is no finer poem in the world. In Psalm 68, with its splendid theme of the triumph of God over His enemies, all the kingdoms of the earth are called upon to sing to God, "who rides in the heavens, the ancient heavens" (32–33).

We find references to the creative activity of God and to His wise government of His creation scattered in many psalms—33: 6–9; 102: 25–28; 147: 15–18. In Psalms 1 and 23, the everyday, pastoral aspects of Nature form the background—trees beside the river, green pastures, quiet waters, gloomy glens. But the fullest treatment of the theme is in Psalms 8, 19, 29, 65, 104, 107, 147, 148. In Psalm 8, it is recognized that man's dominion over Nature is the gift of God to him, and his glory and honour lie in the wise and reverent exercise of his God-given dominion. This psalm has been called "the Magna Carta of humanity", for it finds the source of man's greatness and dignity in the fact that he is remembered and visited by the God whose glory is seen in the stars above. It is by the approach of God to man that all man's inborn littleness can be taken away.

Psalm 19 begins with the same theme that God's marvellous works are to be seen day and night wherever we look. But it goes on to say that that selfsame God has put the moral law in man's heart and desires our homage in obedience to that inward law which transforms life for the sinner. The main picture behind Psalm 29 is a thunderstorm, described in a few vivid words (vv. 3, 5, 8, 9), in which the mighty voice of God is to be heard in seven successive peals. All the divine power evident in the storm is in other ways at the disposal of man, "May the Lord give strength to his people! May the Lord bless his people with peace!" (v. 11). Psalm 65 is typical of several psalms which see Nature rejoicing in God's bountiful provision for man's necessities—the valleys singing, the whole earth glad, the full sea roaring, the fields exulting, the trees waving in joy. The man who wrote Psalm 65 had entered into the experience of pardon, prayer and worship, and he is able to see a vital connection between all that and the

45

strength of the mountains, the moving of the tides, the glory of daybreak and the riches of the harvest.

Psalm 18 : 7–19 and Psalm 126 trace the connection between God's power in Nature and man's protection. In Psalms 36 and 107 the agreement of God's character with the marks of His revelation in Nature is traced out, and in the latter is the repeated grand refrain "Let them thank the Lord for his steadfast love, for his wonderful works to the sons of men".

On this whole subject of the revelation of God in Nature, it has to be added that for these psalmists, as for devout people of every age, it is true that they had eyes for the glory of God in Nature because their eyes had been opened to the presence of God in other ways. They found confirmation and enrichment in Nature for what they had already discovered. This is well expressed in the lines of a modern poetess:

> Let me be quiet now and kneel,
> Who never knelt before,
> Here, where the leaves paint patterns light
> On a leaf-strewn forest floor;
> For I, who saw no God at all
> In sea or earth or air
> Baptized by Beauty, now look up
> To see God everywhere.

But, as we shall see later, there are still deeper questions in personal religion to which the revelation in Nature is incapable of supplying an answer.

God in the Nations

The second sphere of God's glory is in the creation, guidance and control of the life of nations. This is an idea which belongs to the essential structure of the Bible, and there is abundant witness to it in the Psalms. The God who is sovereign Creator and Ruler of heaven and earth chooses nations, is present in the unfolding of their history, and has a divine plan and purpose for them. All that He has done in the works of nature finds its place in the larger purposes which are being worked out in history. The "Holy One of Israel" is in the midst of His people (46: 5) and it would be tragedy and terror indeed if He were to remove His presence from among them (89: 38–45).

It should be noted that at least two of the greatest of the Nature Psalms include a reference to God's special relationship to Israel— "He declares his word to Jacob, and statutes and ordinances to Israel. He has not dealt thus with any other nation" (147: 19–20); "He has raised up a horn for his people, praise for all his saints, for the people of Israel who are near to him" (148: 14). Precisely the same emphasis is to be found in such passages as 74: 12–17; 75: 5, 10; 77: 5–20; 80: 8–11; 81: 1–10; 89: 17–24; 92: 10; 96: 12–13; 98: 7–9; 112: 9; 135: 5–12; 136: 4–22. At all these points we touch the vast thought of the transcendent Providence of God. No nation is wholly responsible for or capable of writing its own history, for God is the major factor in every human problem and He has a controlling hand in everything. As we study what the Psalms say about all this, we find that, even when the facts were most forbidding and when the faith in a sovereign Providence was hard to cling to, they were never driven to confusion and despair. The only Psalm which may be the one exception to this is Psalm 88. There are no better examples of confidence against fearful odds, sustained by the final assurance that God does hold the reins, than Psalms 124 and 129, and close behind them 57 and 125.

The Exodus of Israel from Egypt is the second greatest event in the religious history of the human race, the first of course being the coming of Christ. God's election of Israel at the Exodus and His making them His own people by a covenant are dwelt upon with awe and gratitude in lawgivers, historians, prophets and psalmists alike. The choice of Israel was no action of dictatorship on God's part, nor was it an obvious choice on the ground that Israel was a better nation than the others (Deuteronomy 7: 6–9; 9: 4–5). It was the result of God's own inscrutable wisdom and will, His gracious decision to reveal His saving purposes for mankind in and through this people the history of which before the Exodus and still more after the Exodus was peculiarly suited to such purposes. All Israel's history was to be "salvation-history". The glory of the Exodus is the theme of almost twenty of the Psalms—in whole or in part—18, 44, 60, 68, 74, 75, 76, 78, 80, 81, 83, 89, 95, 97, 105, 106, 114, 135, 136—and the common thought which holds them all together is their consciousness of a unique, merciful act of God, in deliverance from the bondage of Egypt, and in the giving of a covenant and a law.

A great part of the revelation of God's glory in history is that He does not forget, but remains faithful to His covenant. On the human side, to forget and to rebel is the all too easy and perilous tendency; and these very words are most prominent in all God's charges, promises and warnings to His people. But on God's side the great word is "remember"—He remembers His covenant—Psalms 105: 42–3; 106: 44–5; 111: 5–6; 136: 23–24. This remembrance will stand to all eternity—"Thy name, O Lord, endures forever: thy renown, O Lord, throughout all ages" (135: 13–14). On the other hand, He expects and values faithfulness to His covenant on man's side. His demand is always

48

for loyal remembrance of it—112: 5–6; 119: 55. The new covenant in the Lord's Supper, also in terms of remembrance, is the final fulfilment of the old covenant of the Exodus. That is a most impressive example of God's control of events of history under His sovereign purpose of redemption.

All God's acts are royal acts, and so this is the point at which to refer to the Royal Psalms. Much study is given nowadays to the conception that kingship in Israel was "sacral", an outward sign, along with the priest and prophet, of God's relationship to His people. In this connection it has frequently been suggested that not a few of the Psalms have to be associated with an Enthronement Festival held once a year as a ceremony of God's accession to His throne, a throne of universal dominion. There is a good deal of uncertainty and speculation in such a theory, and our understanding of the Psalms specially selected as fitting for the occasion is not greatly increased or deepened by the theory. What is certain and all-important is that these Royal Psalms present a conception which is utterly essential to true religion—that supreme authority and rule are with God alone. It is because He is indeed King that He can be trusted as Shield and Saviour. The main Psalms here are 20, 21, 47, 93, 95–100, and also 102: 15; 138: 4. Human brotherhood among the peoples—as in Psalms 67, 87, 145—can be established only on the basis of this sovereign rule of God, by peoples who know and praise Him.

God in Judgment

The third sphere of God's glory is in His judgment of the world. The life of the world has its very dark side. In the plight of sin and evil, man is faced with a problem which he is powerless to solve. According to the Bible, the world created by God has gone disastrously wrong. Man has become a rebel against God, defying what the Creator intended him to be, choosing the opposite of what His Maker said was good. Pride, selfishness and self-glorifying have entered in; and man, the crown of God's creation, has by free choice turned against God. From this tragic fall, every form of evil life comes to the world—strife, conflict, drunkenness, lust, murder. Every relationship is disturbed when the primary relationship with God is broken. Such is the grim picture in the early chapters of Genesis, and it is frankly said that the Creator "was sorry that he had made man upon the earth, and it grieved him to his heart. So the Lord said, I will blot out man whom I have created from the face of the ground" (Genesis 6: 6–7). But the Creator did not proceed with this drastic, final solution. Instead He set Himself the task of putting right what man had put wrong, of making man new. The whole Bible from Genesis 12 to Revelation 22 is the account of God's action to rescue fallen man, unfolded stage by stage to the decisive hour of Christ's coming.

The judgments of God on the sinful world have to be understood against that background. They are not vindictive, bent only on punishment, in nature or purpose, but essentially they reveal the character of a God who is resolved to defeat and destroy evil. Even a Psalm like 145, so full of vigour, joy, praise and confidence in every verse, cannot exclude at the end the words "but all the wicked he will destroy". This is the Psalm to which the Talmud, a Jewish collection of teachings, pays the remarkable tribute, "he who says Psalm 145 three times daily may rest assured that he will inherit eternal life". From the Psalms we learn that "the wicked will not stand in the judgment" (1: 5), that "the earth feared and was still, when God arose to establish judgment" (76: 8–9), that God will judge the earth with righteousness (7:8; 9:8; 10:18; 67:4; 82:8; 96:10; 98:9; 110:6; 135:14). The root idea of all these passages is that God will see justice done, and it will often involve suffering and ruin. The emphasis is sometimes on the nation or nations, and sometimes upon the individual; but it is the same process. As the judgments of God proceed upon their sombre way, the results may often fall upon the innocent as well as the guilty. That is a problem bravely faced in the Psalms, and to be studied in the next chapter. But God never ceases to work for the support of the good and the overthrow of the evil.

There are vivid pictures of how God's judgment operates in passages like 2:9; 3:7; 31:18; 36:12; 59:5; 74:11; 77:16-19; 83:13; 132:18. There is a stern, awful side to God's dealings with men. The psalmists do not conceal this, nor would they regard it as irreconcilable with His mercy and loving kindness. For the fullest teaching of the Psalms on this theme of judgment we have to turn to Psalms 7, 44, 58, 60, 78:17-41; 79; 82, 83, 94.

In Psalm 44 we are led deep into the mystery of God's ways. The writer permits himself to use daring and extravagant language of God, as a slave-dealer who has made a bad bargain (vv. 11-16), thus making his people a laughing-stock, and as an inactive, sleeping God who has to be roused by us (23-26). Although the psalm opens with thanksgiving for victory in the past, there has been a serious relapse and the apparent loss of everything. But although the writer cannot honestly find a cause for God's judgments, he still believes that it is all for the sake of God (vv. 20-22), and that the prayer for deliverance will be heard because of His steadfast love.

Psalm 75 clusters itself around verse 7—"but it is God who executes judgment, putting down one and lifting up another". To join battle with God is a hopeless and cheerless task, for God will maintain the righteous order. He has set up and built it into the very fabric of life (vv. 2–5, 8, 10). In Psalm 76 God's majesty and strength are pictured as a triumphal return from battle (vv. 2–4), paralysing the enemy (5–6). The evil things men do may serve in the end to bring praise to God; and, though He does not compel men, He is able to pull them up at the right time (8–10). In Psalm 78: 17–41, the argument is very clear and forceful, and the sum of it is that God has to teach people by the lessons of their past, the sufferings of which are the just punishments of "the Holy One of Israel", and that He is always resolved to lead His people back, even by dark, hard ways. It is very profitable to study Psalms 44 and 78 together, and to see the contrasts of thought.

Psalm 82 is concise and vivid. It has been held that it is not men who are addressed here, but "sons of gods" in the sense of beings of the unseen world. But it is more likely that the writer has in mind earthly rulers and judges who have failed miserably in their function (2–5); they are summoned to judgment by the Judge from whom there is no escape (6–8). Psalm 58 is closely akin to this. Evil men in high place are condemned, as perverse and obstinate since their very birth, listening to no advice or warning, and seemingly beyond correction (3–6). Such men cannot escape retribution, and so people are aroused to see that there is a Supreme Judge (v. 11). Although it may be somewhat crudely expressed, the meaning of verse 10 is that the judgment of God is something to rejoice in; and this all-important understanding of it appears also in 67: 4; 96: 11–13; 97: 10–12; 98: 7–9. Psalm 94 also opens with a description of God as the "Lord, thou God of vengeance", and finishes with the assurance that He cannot be allied with evil (20–23). He knows and cares all the time, though the wicked may comfort themselves that He does not (5–7). By His judgments God is training His people

(12–15), and for that reason the whole earth should rejoice and have a sure hope in troublous times.

(*ii*) THE EMOTIONS OF THE SOUL

No one can live a normal life upon this earth at any period without being confronted with the range of facts which has been surveyed in the last section. The many-sided manifestations of Nature, often bountiful and beautiful, sometimes terrifying and ugly, the change and chance of the history of peoples and nations, and the heavy impact of catastrophe on the personal, local, national or world-wide scale—all this makes up the total setting of life.

In the age when the Psalms were written and collected, the scope of that setting was more restricted than now. One simple example of this is the fact that in the quiet, simple society of the Old Testament times, there would be many of the people in that small country who never saw Jerusalem or the Temple. The limits of the setting have been immeasurably widened, but in substance it remains the same—Nature around and above us, history continually making its impact upon our life, and ever the visitation of periodic calamity.

The question, however, which separates men into distinct groups is "How far is God evident and at work in this setting?" Do the heavens tell the glory of God and the firmament proclaim His handiwork? When we lift the veil of history, do we see a Sovereign, Personal Will above all other wills? Are we able to read in tragedy and breakdown the judgments of a holy, merciful God? Some sort of personal attitude and response to the total setting, as we see it, is inevitable. It is in this way that the

53

emotions of the soul find expression. The whole circle of these emotions is uttered forth in the Psalms.

In the whole Bible, the good life is the godly life. The wicked man is the man who does not fear God and keep His commandments. The fear of God and respect for His law make a man "upright of heart". Such men have made a covenant with God by sacrifice (50: 5); and there are frequent passages which proclaim God's protection for them (35: 10; 37: 15; 40: 17; 70: 5; 86: 13; 109: 21; 140: 12). This type of man will avoid and scorn the kind of behaviour that the wicked boast in—5: 6; 10: 3; 14: 4; 17: 12; 37: 20; 64: 3; 55: 23; 68: 1; 86: 14; 73: 3 and 12; 101: 5; 140: 5.

There is an amazingly full treatment of personal religion in the Psalms. It is probable that Psalms of this kind make up more than half the collection, and they reach down to a depth which many of the others do not know. The writers of these Psalms have not come by their convictions easily. The marks of tension and struggle are present everywhere. In a phrase, a verse or a group of verses, these writers describe the cause of the tension and struggle; but their only reason for writing the psalm is to state the assurance which they now hold, though it is often assailed and the enemies of their soul never fall and lie stone-dead on the battlefield of life. They have the possession of a certainty which nothing now can undermine. They will not allow what they do not and cannot know to rob them of what they do know. Such psalms arise in one heart and then reach out and lodge in many other hearts. That is the process that goes on whenever the Psalms are used in private devotion or public worship, if true benefit is being derived from these acts.

Gratitude to God is the first emotion which surges up whenever personal religion begins to get warm. "O give thanks to the Lord, for he is good, for his steadfast love endures forever" (Psalm 136: 1), and then that lovely psalm, so suitable for recitation, goes on to review God's action in the creation of heaven, earth, sea and the lights of the sky, followed by His action in Egypt on Israel's behalf and in the wilderness years till He brought them to the land of their inheritance. This Psalm reminds people that the roots of their being are in a long past and, if they only know that past well, they will be filled with thankfulness, and recognize with adoration that He alone does great wonders (v. 4). All that is good and honourable in a nation's past is the doing of the Lord, and it is not different within the individual's experience. The oft-repeated refrain of this psalm reminds us that the unchanging essence of God's nature is steadfast love.

Probably most of these writers have no clear faith in a future life, but that does not prevent them from making the very most of the opportunity of this life and being grateful for it—"I will give thanks to thee forever" (30: 12), but he had already asked in verse 9 "What profit is there in my death, if I go down to the Pit; will the dust praise thee, will it tell of thy faithfulness?" "In death there is no remembrance of thee, in the grave who can give thee praise?" (6: 5). The writer of Psalm 35, telling of his danger and hopelessness and pleading with God to intervene and stand up for him (vv. 22–25), and now in the happy position of reporting that God has indeed delivered him, declares "I will thank thee in the great congregation; in the mighty throng I will praise thee. My tongue shall tell of thy righteousness and of thy praise all the day long" (vv. 18, 28). In Psalm 107, which opens with the same call to give thanks, after each section describing a very different situation of need or anxiety, he adds the same resonant refrain "Let them thank the Lord for his steadfast love, for his wonderful works to the sons of men" (9, 15, 21, 31)—expanded in two cases to make sure that the thanksgiving be made in the worship of the congregation. Gratitude is only partial if it is kept wholly personal and does not send the worshipper to the place where others gather to pray and praise.

It is this joy in thanksgiving that we have to read into the references in the Psalms to the dance, which in a ritual sense has a long history in Israel (Exodus 15: 20; Judges 11: 34; 1 Samuel 18: 6; Judges 21: 19–21; 2 Samuel 6: 14–16; 1 Kings 18: 26). The two closing Psalms of the collection include the dance along with all the instruments of music (149: 3; 150: 4). The term "bless" is used in the Old Testament in two senses—it is something that God does to man, and it is something that man is expected to do to God. "Stand up and bless the Lord your God from everlasting to everlasting. Blessed be thy glorious name which is exalted above all blessing and praise" (Nehemiah 9: 4–5). Every day brings its own reasons for it (145: 2) and so will it be while life lasts (63: 4).

The finest example of this in the Psalms is 103. If we do not forget God's benefits, His forgiveness, His healing, His crowning, satisfying, wonderful mercy, His establishing of a steadfast throne in heaven, we shall call upon our soul and all that is within us to bless His holy name, and to share in the blessing that goes on in all His dominions.

Psalm 118 is another glorious example. It opens and closes with the same call "O give thanks". Its author has passed through great distress, because he has been let down by the men in whom he trusted (vv. 5–9), and the attack of his foes was widespread and fierce (vv. 10–13). The victory, however, has come through "the right hand of the Lord", "the Lord's doing and marvellous in our eyes", and the rest of the psalm deals with his thanksgiving in the place of worship—"we bless you from the house of the Lord". The imagery of these closing verses—15, 19, 20, 26, 27—is that of worship in public ceremony. Two verses of this psalm—22 and 26—are applied to Christ in Matthew 21: 9 and 42. The theme of thanksgiving can be pursued further in Psalms 18, 30, 32, 34, 40, 41, 66, 92, 124, 129, 138. There is no finer and more fruitful way of expressing gratitude to God for what He has done in our own life than by letting others into the secret, especially those of the younger generation—"Come, O sons, listen to me, I will teach you the fear of the Lord" (34: 11); "Come and hear, all you who fear God, and I will tell what he has done for me" (66: 16).

Resistance to God

Resistance to the Will of God is an all too common emotion of the heart, even when man is confronted by the glory disclosed in Nature, History and Judgment. This attitude is indeed universal. The teaching of the Bible on the nature of man is that he has been made in the image of God, which means that he is endowed with a capacity for getting to know God. At one and the same time man craves that fulness of life which can be attained only in the knowledge of God and yet offers a radical resistance to the approach of God. Such is the human dilemma with its hope and tragedy, its possibilities of great blessing or great ruin.

When Paul unfolds this basic doctrine of man in Romans 3: 10–14, he supports the dark side of his argument by reference to certain very gloomy verses in the Psalms—14: 1-3; 5: 9; 140: 3; 10: 7; 36: 1. All these references stress how deep transgression is in man's heart, though some of them refer more to what a man sees in others rather than what he knows to be equally in himself.

In Psalm 1, which sets reverence for God's law in the forefront of the Psalm, the very first verse is set in a form which suggests that man's resistance to God is a thing that grows and grows and that man can get dangerously accustomed to it. The wicked man begins by *walking* in the counsel of the wicked, then he comes to *stand* in the way of sinners, and finally he *sits* in the seat of the scorners. Standing is a worse condition than walking in these matters, and sitting is worse than standing. The inborn opposition to God has increased when a man who starts with walking in evil ways gets to like them so much that he stands in them, and it has gone a stage further when he no longer even stands but sits down, in comfortable, settled ease with his way of life. The process is one of deterioration, of gradually getting worse, and it is too frequently allowed to work itself out—unless it be arrested and reversed by the other radical element in man's nature which craves for God.

The teaching of Psalm 14 (repeated in 53) is in place here. It is mainly an account of the results that follow when men persuade themselves in their heart that there is no God. Men never succeed in completely persuading themselves in their head that there is no God. There is always the margin of doubt and uncertainty, but it is not theoretical atheism but practical atheism which is spoken of here. Very bluntly, the man who sets himself to live as if there was no God, though he can never prove that, is described as a fool. It is the root error, and the worst form of human resistance to the Higher Will. Two other types in the Bible are held up to scorn as fools—the man who believes that

58

this material world is everything (Luke 12: 20), and the Christian who thinks that the physical body passes into heaven (1 Corinthians 15: 35–50). No one is born an atheist, and atheists are made in different ways. Sometimes it is by the proud worship of the intellect, sometimes by taking life too lightly and at surface-level only, sometimes by the wrong attitude of rebellion to trouble, sometimes by the poor, distorted witness of believers, sometimes by a guilty conscience that will not seek the way of peace. But the main way is as in this Psalm—absorption in immediate gain and pleasure, a way of life to which the idea of God is inconvenient and distasteful. This way makes for the destroying of the very foundations (11 : 3). God has His own ways of showing its emptiness (73 : 18–20).

Trust in God

Trust in God, though difficult enough to maintain, is as deep an emotion as man is capable of. The whole life of prayer is possible as the natural, necessary expression of trust. This is a leading conception in the Psalms. "Trust in him at all times, O people; pour out your heart before him: God is a refuge for us" (62: 8). This embodies a very high demand, "at all times" and few reach it. But those who do so find out that there are gains in losses, advantages in disadvantages, victories in defeats. These people assume that God's promises are reliable, not reckless, and that He has given no absurd or extravagant guarantees. They have had before them the good example of others who have trusted and honoured God under great handicaps. All life's losses and misfortunes look different to a godly man.

For the psalmist's trust in God is usually associated with two convictions—one about man, one about God. Man is a being of utter dependence on God. "Put them in fear, O Lord! Let the nations know that they are but men" (9: 20). Man will not prevail when God arises to judge (v. 19). These verses are at the end of a psalm of great thanksgiving for a deliverance that was beyond human wisdom and power. Man is thought of here in his essential, natural weakness and helplessness apart from God—what Wesley's hymn calls "Adam's helpless race". Providence sometimes works in a rough way to convince man of this. All that is good in man too has its source in God. On the other hand, trust is drawn out and matured by the assurance that God, for all His greatness and majesty, desires our trust and prayer, and has given us the instinct for both. When the Psalms appeal to man to trust God, they do not neglect to proclaim as an aid to trust— "The Lord, the Most High, is terrible, a great king over all the earth" (47: 2). "Great is the Lord and greatly to be praised" (48: 1). "For thou art great and doest wondrous things, thou alone art God" (86: 10). In the realm He governs, the part He plays in man's life and the purposes He has in view, His greatness shines, drawing men to Him. This God also takes delight in us— "The Lord takes pleasure in his people" (149: 4; 147: 11). It is so easy to think of what God dislikes in us. But it is a Bible insight, neglected perhaps, that God also finds pleasure in us, in our natural talents when they are used well, in our capacity for goodness and sacrifice, in our possibilities of repentance and dedication.

"Lead thou me to the rock that is higher than I" (61: 2). Man's littleness and his greatness lie side by side here. He is in continual need of a shelter, and the only shelter is the Rock higher than himself; but the only Rock higher than man himself is God—"Thou art my refuge, a strong tower against the enemy" (61: 3). All prayer proceeds from this—"Call upon me in the day of trouble; I will deliver you, and you shall glorify me" (50: 15).

In the Psalms there is a strange absence of prayers of intercession for other people, of the kind found in 28: 9, "save thy people, and bless thy heritage". But prayer of every other type is plentifully illustrated in them. A very high degree of faith in God is found in 18: 1–3, 49–50—at the opening and close of a psalm which in the main is devoted to a vivid, detailed review of the experiences which are illuminated by such a faith. In Psalm 55, a man who has every cause to be downcast tells that it is by believing and regular prayer that he is lifted up. Psalm 27 is a peculiar treasure in personal religion. Its writer knows that out of his own past he can draw the assurance that God will continue in future to be his comfort and light. He has entered into an experience closer than the closest human relationships (v.10) and, so long as he is in the land of the living, he will discover more deeply its value and power. In Psalm 116, tender and moving, a man who had been right in the depths testifies to the power of prayer. For him the one right thing now is to go on praying, winning by prayer a serene mind and a quiet heart (vv. 7–9), and inspired by prayer to an open, public testimony of his debt to God (vv. 12–19). There is much to be learned on prayer in Psalms 140–143, but Psalm 116 is unsurpassed for its insights on this subject. Other Psalms on prayer are 5, 6, 28, 40, 56, 57, 63, 64, 77, 86, 102, 120, 130.

Penitence Before God

Penitence before God is an absolutely necessary condition for a growing personal experience of Him. It has often been said that the Psalter as a whole is somewhat lacking in its emphasis on repentance; and there is some evidence indeed that protestations of innocence before God are too numerous, e.g. 7: 8; 17: 1; 18: 23; 44: 17–18; 26: 1; 59: 3; 101: 2. There is a place for this in respect of a particular situation for which the individual may wrongly be held to be responsible—but in the wider general sense there is never justification for it. Men in every age have found it hard and uncongenial to accept the fact that sin is exceedingly serious and that it is in them all in that form. From this it follows that profound repentance is always likely to be a comparatively rare experience, as also the joy, peace and inspiration of forgiveness.

There are seven Psalms which have been called the Penitential Psalms—6, 32, 38, 51, 102, 130, 143. The noblest of these is 51, with 38 a good second. In Psalms 6 and 102 there is little direct reference to sin. The burden of Psalm 32 is not confession but joy in the experience of pardon, and it is somewhat similar in 130, in which the two great thoughts are that no man can stand before God if He gave him his strict deserts, and that there is a force at work in the experience of forgiveness which helps to make the forgiven man a God-fearing, that is, a good man (130: 3–4). Because of these assurances, he can go on trusting, waiting and hoping (vv. 5–8). There is a close relationship between penitence and gratitude. This connection meant a great deal to a people, like the people of the Old Testament Church, who believed that in the system of animal sacrifices there was an atonement only for sins which were done unwittingly (Numbers 15: 22–29) and not for deliberate, high-handed offences (Numbers 15: 30–34). There is an echo of this in Psalm 18: 27, "the haughty eyes thou dost bring down", where the adjective conveys the same idea of proud and intentional sin. The psalmists, with all the backing of the great prophets on this matter as on most others, teach that all forms of sin are covered by the divine mercy offered to and made its own by genuine repentance.

Some of the Psalms in this group regard bodily trouble or adversity as the evidence that the sufferer, oneself or another, is indeed a sinner. This is the mistake against which the Book of Job strikes so hard, and it was rejected by Jesus Christ (Luke 13 : 4; John 9: 2–12). This serious misconception does not tinge Psalm 51. It is well worthy to be called "confession of the purest sort". Its prayer for inward renewal (v. 10) is as deep and necessary a prayer as it is possible for man to make. If that door can be opened, many other closed doors of stubborn temptation, mistaken values, selfish ambitions, and broken relationships will soon open also. It is the divine, creative action which gives man the new, clean heart, not "the labours of our hands" nor the stirrings of our wills. Joy, then, returns to the life which knows that it is safe with God; and with joy a willing, generous spirit (v. 12). He also gets a quickened sense of responsibility to let other people know so that they too may be converted (vv. 13, 15). Finally, his sharing in the acts of public worship becomes sincere and acceptable (vv. 16–19).

There are remarkable results to follow in a man's life from "knowing my transgressions and having my sin ever before me" (v. 3) and his humble recognition that all his sin is primarily against God (v. 4). This could suggest a morbid sense of sin haunting a man everywhere at all times. But it is a blessing to have such a sense of sin if it reminds us of what we have been rescued from, what we might have become had we not been so rescued, if it makes us very careful about our future life, if it helps us to be more ready to forgive others, and if it keeps fresh in the soul the sense of the everlasting mercy which is our only hope.

It might cast a new light on the study of these Psalms, if it were remembered that the Church for long periods associated them with the seven deadly sins—6 with anger, 32 with pride, 38 with gluttony, 51 with luxury, 102 with avarice, 130 with envy, 143 with sloth.

Obedience to God

Obedience to the Will of God is a further emotion of the soul, closely interlinked with gratitude and penitence. Gratitude turns obedience into a joy, "thy statutes have been my songs in the house of my pilgrimage" (119: 54). Penitence changes the inward attitude and motive, "I will run in the way of thy commandments when thou enlargest my understanding" (119: 32). Many people happily discover and are ready to confess that the trouble which they have often had in not hearing God's voice was caused by an unwillingness to hear, a sort of convenient deafness in their personal life. There is a strong element of challenge in the Psalms, especially those whose theme is the Law. Outward actions of worship are no substitute for obedience, but they ought to provide a much-needed drive towards obedience. It belongs to God to command, and to men to obey, not to argue, protest, deny or rebel. By obedience we attain to moral righteousness, and without that all ritual is empty, misleading and dangerous. The Law is God's gift to assist men towards right behaviour. In the greatest of the Law Psalms, it is said, "I hate double-minded men, but I love thy law. Depart from me, you evildoers, that I may keep the commandments of my God" (119: 113, 115). "The Lord loves those who hate evil" (97: 10).

In Israel the commandments of God come both to the nation and the individual. The Psalms which chiefly deal with this subject are 1, 15, 19 (7–11), 26, 40, 52, 112, 119. It is by a careful, significant design that the Psalter is introduced by a short, lucid Psalm which tells men that there are two ways to choose from— the way of delight in the law of the Lord or the way of rejection of the law of the Lord. The former way is the way of happiness. This implies that the restraints of God's law are not fetters or burdens but a source of vitality and gladness, as an unfailing fountain (vv. 2–3). This idea is expanded in Psalm 19: 7–11. Throughout the entire length of 119, the love of God's law, His instruction, His Word is presented as a source of joy, guidance and strength. The Psalms come to us out of a world in which God's chosen people were all too prone to abandon His cove- nant and to enter into alliances with other peoples which were damaging to their religion and often led to apostasy (deserting God). All the Law-Psalms call the wanderers—and all the modern wanderers too—to the Law which was part and parcel of the covenant at Mount Sinai. At our best we are straying sheep, and for this reason the greatest psalm of the Law ends, "Let me live, that I may praise thee, and let thy ordinances help me. I have gone astray like a lost sheep; seek thy servant, for I do not forget thy commandments" (119: 175–176).

The Seasons of Darkness

Depression in an evil, baffling world is still another emotion of the soul. There are seasons when doubt and darkness visit men of faith. It is indeed true that it is men of very deep faith who can enter upon occasion furthest into these dark nights of the soul. The kind of depression which visits people who have little faith is a light thing compared with this. Times come when it is hard for His saints to feel sure that they are indeed in God's hands (Deuteronomy 33: 3), as if there could be no doubt that He was holding them fast and safe. If men could always be sure of that with an unclouded conviction, there would be in their life indeed the quietness and confidence which give peculiar strength. It is not always obvious that "light dawns for the righteous, and joy for the upright in heart" (97: 11). Experiences have to be faced when the shelter of the Higher Rock cannot be reached, when the glory of God is obscured, when gratitude seems a mockery, when penitence brings no peace, when obedience seems valueless.

There is a great deal in the Psalms on this hard subject. For all its complex difficulties, no psalmist yields to fatalism or despair, except possibly the writer of 88. The others which grapple with the problems of evil and calamity are very noble Psalms. In Psalm 55, there is a verse which goes so far as to say that there is a special blessedness in change and misfortune, and that the reason why some people do not fear God is that they have not had enough of this sort of experience (v. 19). (The rendering of the Revised Standard Version, "because they keep no law" may well miss the point here.) It is a thought which has a parallel in Deuteronomy 32: 11, Jeremiah 48: 11, and even in the words of Christ in John 16: 7. There are two conflicting attitudes to the changes of life—extreme dislike and extreme love of it. But God has His big purposes to be effected through change and dislocation, and the things which disturb us can do us and the world great good, driving us back to what can never change.

Psalms 42–43 have a very clear word to say on the subject of depression, for which there is no quick and easy remedy. This writer has felt the dark shadow come over him, wave upon wave—"All thy waves and thy billows have gone over me" (42: 7). His faith is shaken and tried. He is far away from the place he loves, and he is hindered from taking part in the worship of which he was once a leader, and he is taunted by cruel people who mock his faith in God. He is almost overwhelmed by it all. It is notable that his absence from the familiar place of worship is a main element in his dejection. But the loss of faith and hope is life's saddest and heaviest loss, and that he has not experienced, for he still has his hope in God, for "I shall again praise him, my help and my God" (42: 11). The light and truth of God for which he prays will bring him again to "thy holy hill and to thy dwelling. Then I will go to the altar of God, to God my exceeding joy" (43: 3-4).

The Psalms which are devoted altogether to this problem are 11, 12, 13, 31, 37, 49, 73, 77. Naturally none of them can offer a complete solution to it, else faith would have no place, and faith would have ceased to be a battle. Faith is not a watertight solution of mysteries, but a resolute holding on despite all the appearances. In this the psalmists were supported by reflection on what they believed God had already done and on the very faculties He had given them as human beings (94: 8-10). None of these Psalms has reached up to the level found in the New Testament at which men can rejoice in tribulation, and that is not to be looked for.

The writer of Psalm 11 is a brave and defiant man, and he scorns the suggestion of a cowardly flight from his difficulties, for that is of no true benefit either to himself or others whom he influences. In Psalm 12 a man well advanced in years looks back and around and sees many sad changes, but he feels sure that God's word can be relied on, and that He will settle accounts with evildoers. In Psalm 13 the writer struggles out of despair into new hope. For him the hiding of God's face now seems more apparent than real, and all through the dark time God had been providing for him liberally. Psalm 31 is one of conflicting

67

feelings and perplexities, and should be read alongside Psalm 6. It has very sacred associations with the Cross of Christ (Luke 23 : 46). Its author can still pray with a sense of reality for deliverance and protection; and the closing verses (19-24) are full of thanksgiving for the expected answer.

"Fretting is as bad as swearing", said John Wesley. Indeed it is another form of swearing. But the author of Psalm 37 is almost too simple and confident in the way he seeks to dispose of the problem of the prosperity of the wicked. His main argument is that it is only a matter of time till they will be cast down and his own prosperity restored. But he is not mistaken in his conviction that bad men have no sure hold on anything that abides, and that that is so because God is just and good.

Psalm 49 (like 78) is given in a form of "parable" or "riddle" (vv. 3-4). He is to reveal with the help of the "lyre" hidden things of deep importance. His main problem seems to be great wealth in the hands of those who use it badly, arousing jealousy in the hearts of the poor; and the two lines of his solution are that wealth is swiftly-passing and futile, and that righteousness is proved right in the end.

The greatest Psalm of this group is 73 which goes considerably beyond 49. The writer here feels acutely the uselessness of good behaviour (vv. 13-14), and he is finding it hard to keep his feet (vv. 2-3). It is apparently not so much that great trouble has crashed into his own life, but he sees all around the arrogance and security of the wicked (vv. 4-9). He is held back from speaking aloud of his dark perplexity, for this might be disloyal to the good people of the past and upsetting to the faith of good people in the present who did not feel the problem so acutely. But in worship (v. 17) he is given the insight he requires. It comes in two forms —that the prosperity of the wicked is an empty, passing show (vv. 17-20), and the deep solace of his own close relationship to a God who holds his hand (vv. 23–28). This writer had found his way out of darkness into light and peace before he started to write the psalm, and so he opens it with words of buoyant conviction.

In Psalm 77, a very depressed man is getting no help from his prayers nor from his own religious experience up-to-date (vv. 1–4). But he is able to look away from himself and his prayers to his people's long and troubled past—"I consider the days of old, I remember the years long ago" (v. 5). "I will call to mind the deeds of the Lord, yea, I will remember thy wonders of old" (vv. 11–12). "Has God forgotten to be gracious?" he asks (v. 9), and he answers by going back to Jacob, Joseph and the Exodus. There is a great tonic for drooping spirits in a right knowledge of history.

This section may close with a brief glance at two other Psalms. Psalm 4 is a good psalm for the end of the day, showing how a good man reaches the end of the day. Psalms 3 and 4 have often been regarded as designed for royal sacrifices at morning and evening worship. As night comes down, sinful anger should subside, and the opportunity be taken for self-communing as we go to bed (4:4). That should convince a man that his faith in God is a deeper joy than those men have who possess abundance of grain and wine. So "in peace I will both lie down and sleep, for thou alone, O Lord, makest me dwell in safety".

Psalm 71 is a psalm for old age. It is not unlike 69, but it does not have the weariness of spirit which that psalm shows. There is vigour and happiness in it. The old man's prayer is "Do not cast me off in the time of old age; forsake me not when my strength is spent. O God, from my youth thou hast taught me, and I still proclaim thy wondrous deeds; so even to old age and grey hairs, O God, do not forsake me" (vv. 9, 17–18). His experience of God has been lifelong, and there is no better foundation upon which to build up hope. God will never dismiss a man like this. The goodness and mercy of past years will abide to the end.

(*iii*) WHERE OUR HOPE LIES

The study of this aspect of the Psalms has to begin with a difficult, obscure and heavily veiled illustration of how hope may survive in the hearts of sorely-tried men. From it, we can move on to the brighter and richer manifestations of hope. The basic conviction of religion that God is set against all evil and resolved to overcome it will, in certain extreme circumstances, take the form that God may decide that there is no course open except to crush evil and evildoers. This is never an easy conception to manage and control without mistaking some of its meaning.

There is a group of Psalms hard to understand. They have been an offence to many, and have even been a weapon in the hand of the scorner to prove that the God of the Old Testament is a cruel, changeable tyrant, unworthy of respect. These Psalms, therefore, while deserving much reflection in private, can scarcely be used in public worship without careful explanation lest the very thought of God be sadly distorted.

The Imprecatory Psalms

The Imprecatory or Cursing Psalms are five—7, 35, 69, 109, 137. There is not the same degree of fierce vindictiveness in them all, and that reaches its height in 109 and the closing verses of 137. Other Psalms include isolated verses of this kind—2: 9;

18: 37, 40–42; 21: 9–10; 52: 5–6; 59: 10–13; 83: 9–18; 118: 10–12; 129: 6–7; 139: 21–22. In Psalms where it is hardly to be expected, it is found—101: 3, 8; 149: 6–9. Outside the Psalter also such passages are to be met—speaking of curses which fall not only on Israel's enemies but on Israel too—Deuteronomy 27: 15–26; Leviticus 26: 14–39; Isaiah 34: 9–11; Jeremiah 48: 10; Ezekiel 35. Terrible prayers for vengeance appear throughout the Old Testament—Jeremiah 17: 18 and 18: 21–23; Joshua 10: 13; Judges 16: 28; Nehemiah 4: 5. "Let their own table before them become a snare; let their sacrificial feasts be a trap. Let their eyes be darkened, so that they cannot see. . . May their camp be a desolation, let no one dwell in their tents" (Psalm 69: 22–25). "Let his prayer be counted as sin; may his days be few; may his children be fatherless and his wife a widow; may his children wander about and beg; may they be driven out of the ruins they inhabit. Let there be none to extend kindness to him, nor any to pity his fatherless children" (109: 7–12). The writer of Psalm 137 who begins with poignant memories of Jerusalem now in ruins and is unable to forget Edom's part in that tragedy, feels that he must say of the descendants of these wicked and cruel people, "Happy shall he be who takes your little ones and dashes them against the rock." It is probable that we in the twentieth century which has perpetrated more cruelty than any other and sent many millions of innocent helpless people and their children wandering homeless in the world may not find it too hard to understand such expressions of deep revulsion against heartless tyrants and monsters. There is a special test for faith in singing the Lord's song in a strange land.

It must not be overlooked, as we ponder the problem of these Psalms and wonder how they can be an inspired revelation of the Spirit of God, that they were chosen by the cult-prophets who collected the Psalter, for inclusion in it. This was for a higher

71

purpose than as examples of "hymns of hate", mere expressions of and incentives to personal spite. Various methods have been adopted to explain away these Psalms—by devices of grammar, by interpreting them as allegories, by suggestions that the enemies referred to are not human beings but demonic spirits. But the real justification for their presence in the Psalms is that they bear witness to an aspect of truth which must not ever be neglected—though they do so in a strange, extravagant way.

There is by God's appointment a principle of retribution which never ceases to work in life. This is one of "the stately dependabilities" of life; the consequences have to be faced. Many who have suffered as these writers apparently did have been able to rise above their vindictive feelings and have refused to express their feelings in curses. But that does not alter the fact of retribution. When we are faced with outrageous facts, with behaviour which would destroy the very foundations of life as God has made them, there must be room for the reaction of intense moral indignation. That is what these Psalms really mean. Too often, however, frail men under deep emotion have been unable to separate between moral indignation and personal vengeance. These Psalms err in that way. There is much in the Bible which is not to be taken literally, but must be taken seriously. The words of these Psalms are more profitable for reproof than for doctrine, and yet there is doctrine in them, necessary to a full doctrine of God.

These Psalms, of course, do bring us in their spirit into a realm very different from the Sermon on the Mount and the Cross of Jesus. This is a central, decisive fact; and it means that there is no way to conquer the vindictive spirit than by the supernatural power available in Jesus Christ. It is very significant that, when He stood up to read in the synagogue at Nazareth (Luke 4 : 16–20) announcing His own programme for the Kingdom, He chose as his text the words of Isaiah 61 : 1–4. But He did not read the words "and the day of vengeance of our God" (61 : 2); instead, He closed the book.

This is not to deny that vengeance belongs to God, but Christ's action does outlaw the vindictive spirit. Vengeance is such a dangerous, deadly weapon that it cannot safely be put into men's hands but left to God (Romans 12 : 19–21). On the other hand, it would be false to argue that the Christ who demanded of His followers that God must be put first, even if that meant "hating" our families, did not understand and accept what Old Testament writers were striving, sometimes crudely, to express.

The Message of Hope

From all this we turn to what the Psalter says in contrast to it all. Is there another way? Can we have a hope for a better world here and now? Do we meet Christ anywhere in the Psalms? In many of the Psalms there is a hope for the future of the nation which shines brightly. There are few, if any, of them that consent to the view that all human affairs and prospects are in the end "vanity of vanities". The note is also strongly sounded that this hope is for the whole world, because the God of Israel is the God Who rules all peoples, though as yet they do not know that or recognize Him. The psalmists, like the prophets, teach that there is a law for all mankind given by God. From that it follows that His reign is destined to be universal. This is indeed a great hope, and it is associated in the mind of psalmists and prophets with the vision of an Ideal King who would have a mission greater than any earthly king, however great and good, could fulfil. "May all kings fall down before him, all nations serve him" (72: 11).

There were times when devout people saw Christ in every Psalm. That view has largely disappeared, except in the general sense that the Psalms form a central part of the whole body of Old Testament Scriptures which point forward to a Coming One. We know now that the only true way to grasp the Bible as a whole is to realize that Old Testament and New Testament, for all their many-formed diversity, of date, background, language, literary type and spiritual insight, are made one in Christ.

In the Psalms now to be considered we have the very climax of the message of hope for this world. There are at least five psalms which are Messianic in outlook (looking ahead to the Messiah or Anointed Leader to come)—2, 22, 72, 110 and 132; and in many other places we meet the same thought, e.g. 8: 2, 9; 18: 4–6, 43–50; 21: 13; 45: 6–7; 62: 11–12; 67: 2, 6–7; 68: 16–19; 69: 1–9, 30–32; 70: 3–4; 85: 6–13; 86: 2–4, 16; 89: 35–37; 126: 3–6; 145: 11–13. Outside the Psalms, the great passages to consult are Isaiah 7: 10–16; 9: 1–16; 11: 1–9; 61: 1–4; Micah 5: 2–7; Jeremiah 23: 5–6; 33: 15–16; Zechariah 9: 9–10. Throughout this whole splendid range of daring thought, the picture is of a God who has a positive, triumphant way of overcoming evil. Such thought is far beyond the level of the Cursing Psalms, and indeed the Cursing and the Messianic Psalms seem to be included as examples of two sharply-contrasted ways in which God can be thought of as dealing with the vast problem of evil.

The word "Messiah" is not used as a title by itself in the Old Testament, with the possible exception of a difficult passage in Daniel 9: 25–26. But all that that word now signifies is present in the passages noted. Their writers probably were saying something bigger and truer than they knew at the time. As we look back to what they said from our wider vantage-point in history, we can be confident that it has all been perfectly fulfilled in Christ. Though it is beyond our subject, it may be added that the further thought of the achievement of a mission through suffering, set forth in the Suffering Servant passages—Isaiah 42: 1–4; 44: 2–5; 45: 1–7, 20–25; 49: 1–6; 50: 4–9; 52: 13 to 53: 12—is also perfectly and finally fulfilled in Him. The thoughts of many readers of the Psalms are directed to the conception of the Suffering Messiah not only in the great Psalm 22, but also in 13, 28, 35, 40, 41, 55, 69 and 102. It is by the coming of the Ideal Ruler, by His power and His suffering, that the hope is to be fulfilled that all nations shall bow before the God of Israel, and Israel is intended to be the instrument of God's choice for this high end—8: 1; 22: 27–28; 33: 14; 46: 10; 47: 2, 8, 9; 66: 7; 86: 9; 96: 13; 98: 9; 99: 2; 102: 22; 113: 4; 117: 1; 150: 6. In the worship of the Christian Church many of these Psalms are connected specially with Ascension Day, the victorious crowning of Christ which holds open the door of hope for mankind until God has completed His dealings with mankind in Christ's return in great glory.

Psalm 2 opens with the description of a troubled and rebellious world and ends with an appeal to rulers and princes to seek the one sure way out of this evil, dangerous condition by surrender to the King—"Now therefore, O kings, be wise; be warned, O rulers of the earth. Serve the Lord with fear, with trembling kiss his feet" (vv. 10–11). The translation "kiss ye the Son" may not be reliable, for the original text is very uncertain. But the reference to the Son is clearer in verse 7; and there is also the reference to "his anointed" in verse 2. The assurance at the heart of the Psalm is that it is a foolish and futile thing for man to rebel against God with any hope of winning. That brings upon itself the divine scorn and laughter—"he who sits in the heavens laughs; the Lord has them in derision" (v. 4). God's purpose is to secure a universal dominion for His Son—"ask of me, and I will make the nations your heritage, and the ends of the earth your possession" (v. 8). It is not for an earthly ruler to accomplish this. Christ is not restricted by nation or race, but has a redemptive relationship to all men.

The Universal Messiah

This universal significance of the Messiah is beautifully expressed in 72. "May he have dominion from sea to sea, and from the River to the ends of the earth" (v. 8). This is an Old Testament equivalent to Acts 1: 8, "You shall be my witnesses in Jerusalem and in all Judaea and Samaria and to the end of the earth". This psalm brings us into a spacious realm of thought, in stark contrast to the book of Ezra. Peace and righteousness mark the reign of the Messiah (vv. 1–7), and compassion on the weak and needy whose just cause He upholds (vv. 12–14); the very bounty of the earth will show unusual fertility (v. 16). It is by the gift and favour of God that the Messiah has His universal dominion (v. 1)—a thought which is re-echoed in 18: 43; 20: 6; 21: 1–6; 45: 2–7. This all comes to pass in the hoped-for and prayed-for day.

> Jesus shall reign where'er the sun
> Doth his successive journeys run;
> His Kingdom stretch from shore to shore
> Till moons shall wax and wane no more.

All just and beneficent rule must be drawn out from the rule of God's Son.

Psalm 132 emphasizes that the Lord has made a solemn promise to king David—"The Lord swore to David a sure oath, from which he will not turn back. One of the sons of your body I will set on your throne" (v. 11). But the earlier verses of the psalm (1–10) have made it clear that David was indeed the kind of man to whom such a promise would be most likely made—a man deeply devoted to God's worship, and concerned that there be a worthy place for it to be offered. There was a vow and covenant on David's part, and it is matched by a vow and covenant on God's part—God's answer to the king's prayer. In its build-up and emphasis, Psalm 132 closely resembles Psalm 89. The people over whom David reigns are one with him in his pious desires and dreams. But the closing verses of the psalm bring us to a Zion which is to be "my resting place forever" (v. 14)—to a fuller and more distant realization of the promises than any worldly kingdom can ever offer.

Psalm 22 is very close to the Suffering Servant passages of Isaiah. It has most sacred associations because of its use by Christ upon the Cross (Mark 15: 34). This Psalm (with which 89: 38–52 should be compared) and the Servant passages together give the most moving prophetic portrait of the sufferings of Christ in body and in spirit and of the victory that followed. In verses 1–21 there is a picture of distress and loneliness, and in verses 22–31 the assurance that God has been with him all the time so that there is abundant cause for gratitude and faith. It is upon the same Messianic note of universal dominion that the Psalm ends—"All the ends of the earth shall remember and turn to the Lord; and all the families of the nations shall worship before him. For dominion belongs to the Lord, and he rules over the nations. Yea, to him shall all the proud of the earth bow down; before him shall bow all who go down to the dust, and he who cannot keep himself alive. Posterity shall serve him; men

77

shall tell of the Lord to the coming generation, and proclaim his deliverance to a people yet unborn, that he has wrought it" (vv. 27–31). How different is the mood here from the first part of the Psalm! The writer is so confident in God that he describes the hoped-for deliverance as already an accomplished fact. When the Messiah of God suffers, there can be no ultimate defeat, but only final victory.

Psalm 110 is referred to often in the New Testament—Matthew 22 : 44; Acts 2 : 34–35; Hebrews 1 : 13; 5 : 6; 7 : 17. It moves in the same circle of ideas as the Royal Psalms—the enthronement of the king and the overthrow of his enemies. But this King is also a Priest—"You are a priest forever after the order of Melchizedek" (v. 4).

In a deep sense, Melchizedek can be regarded as the greatest figure before Christ. He passes quickly over the stage of history. At a critical point in history, when Abraham was proud with victory, he is met by Melchizedek to whom he gives tithes (Genesis 14). He comes down from his hill-top town, bearing gifts, seeking guests to serve, and not waiting till they come to him. In Hebrews 5–7 the comparison between Melchizedek and Christ is worked out—a mysterious figure who is the bringer of bread and wine, who thus exercises royal hospitality, who brings a blessing too as of the superior to the inferior, who stands for a kingdom of righteousness and peace, and who himself a priest of the Most High God points forward to another perfect Priesthood. As Priest he mediates between God and the people, but as king he is the instrument of God for the defeat of God's enemies (Psalm 110 : 5–7). "He will drink from the brook by the way" (v. 7) suggests that, in the course of the struggle, the Messiah who has entered into our human limitations will feel wearied and need this refreshing—a prefiguring of "I thirst" (John 4 : 5–7; 19 : 28). In the Messiah all the Kingly and Priestly as well as the Prophetic functions are combined. So must it be for One who is to be God's special and unique representative and ambassador on earth. As St. Augustine said, "Psalm 110 is small in the number of its words, but great in the weight of its ideas."

The Hope of Immortality

There is much in the Psalms on the subject of death, but it is not so sure if there is much in the Psalms or the Old Testament as a whole on the hope of a future life. If there is a trace of the thought of immortality in the Old Testament, we would expect to find it in some of the deepest Psalms. Even there it is not so much directly stated as involved in the other conceptions of man's close communion with God which these psalms expound. It is along this indirect road that we have to search for it.

The hope of immortality seems closed out altogether in such passages as Psalm 6: 5; 13: 3; 30: 9; 49: 19–20; 55: 23; 88: 4–5; 89: 47–48; 104: 27–29. A specially important passage is 49: 19–20—"man cannot abide in his pomp; he is like the beasts that perish". There is much to be said for the Authorized (King James) version here—"Man that is in honour and understandeth not is like the beasts that perish". This is in keeping with the Old Testament view of man as created in the image of God, with a God-given capacity for understanding and knowing God. If he does not employ that faculty for the appointed purpose, man has no sure hope beyond the beasts. There is so much that is good, generous, chivalrous and pleasant in life, making life tolerable. But all that in itself constitutes no title for immortality. In a new communion with God man receives eternal life as God's gift. The Hebrew word *nephesh* which appears hundreds of times and is

79

often translated "soul" or "living soul" does not mean that man as man, by his very nature, is an immortal being. The same word may be used of man in Genesis 2:7 and then of beasts, birds and creeping things; Genesis 1: 20, 24, 30; 9: 12, 15, 16; Ezekiel 47: 9. The last verse of Psalm 49 is saying in a negative way what Jesus Christ says in a positive way in John 17: 3—"This is eternal life, that they know thee the only true God, and Jesus Christ whom thou hast sent."

The general picture of life after death in the Old Testament is sombre enough. The dead are left by God, and He does no wonders where they are (88: 10, 12). In contrast to the joyful gates of Sion man no longer praises God within the gates of death (9: 13; 107: 10; 115: 17; Job 38: 17). Death is a sleep into which man enters, but the possibility of awaking is not ruled out (17: 15; 73: 20, 23; 139: 7-9). The world into which the dead pass is usually described by the Hebrew word "Sheol" which appears sixty-five times in the Old Testament, sixteen of these being in the Psalms. This word is not to be translated as "hell" in the sense of a state of life where the evil and impenitent are shut off from God forever. It simply means the dwellings of the dead. It is below the earth (Genesis 37; Isaiah 14: 9). It is a place of darkness, silence and shadow, from which there is no return (Genesis 42: 36, 38; Isaiah 26: 14-19; Psalm 83: 10; 88: 7-13; Job 10: 21; 17: 13; Psalm 94: 17; Job 26: 6; 28: 22; 30: 23; 7: 9). On the other hand, a real, active life after death is suggested by passages like 2 Kings 2: 11; Genesis 5: 24; Job 19: 25-27; Isaiah 26: 19; Daniel 12: 2-3.

The constant, reliable protection of God is a favourite theme in the Psalms and many prayers for it are made. The classic example is Psalm 91, and that writer states it with a confidence that is almost excessive, if it is taken too literally. All the main ideas of the psalm suggest personal communion with God. In that experience there is shelter, security and strength, and in that there is sufficient help for all the uncertainties and dangers of life, including death itself. Optimism of that kind can be drawn only from deep, personal communion with God.

It has been already noted that the main problem grappled with in Psalm 73 is the success of the wicked and worldly—but in verses 23–27, introduced by "Nevertheless", he has at least a glimpse of the unseen glory into which he believes, on the ground of the experience of being held here and now by God's hand, he will finally be received. There is the same glimpse in 30: 5, "weeping may tarry for the night, but joy comes with the morning", and in the childlike serenity of 131, a short Psalm of three verses ending on the note of hope "from this time forth and for evermore".

In Psalm 103, the primary theme is not man's mortality, but rather the reasons in personal life and in national history for profound gratitude to God (vv. 1–5, 6–7) for His limitless mercy. But the writer cannot exclude from the picture the thought of the frailty and brevity of human life (vv. 13–18). Where can a man whose thoughts range over such a wide field find a hope in which he can exult except in the very character of the experience of God which he at present enjoys?

Psalm 39 raises the same problem of the prosperity of bad men as 73, and its writer also is aware of how guarded his speech ought to be (vv. 1–2). He too knows how quickly-passing is life, and that has its own bearing on the problem which vexes him (vv. 4–6). Also he has had his own experience of trouble, whatever it was—"it is thou who hast done it; remove thy stroke from me" (vv. 9–10). Hopes are rising with him which this life can never fully meet, and so the last verse of the Psalm can hardly mean that at death he ceases to be, but simply that he will be no more here.

Psalm 90 seems to reflect the meditations of an ageing man.

At its best and longest, life is short (vv. 9–10); but for him that is no cause for despondency. On the contrary, it is a good reason for making the very most of life so that we may get a heart of wisdom (v. 12). As he sees life, it is the scene of suffering caused by our sins (vv. 7–9, 11); and he joins suffering and death together. But the God to whom he prays is superior to time and change, and in fellowship with Him he may hope for a sure dwelling-place, and "the blessing of life for evermore" (133: 3; 61: 7). The final prayer for the "establishing of the works of our hands" has more than an earthly reference.

An Eternal Hope

It is in Psalms 16 and 17 that we reach the supreme expression of the eternal hope which is at the heart of present communion with God. In 16 there is hardly anything said about enemies or about the fear of early death. Like the writer of 27, he is a man of strong trust in God (vv. 1, 7–8) and life has been good to him (vv. 5–6). Such a man can continue to trust God in the hour of death, and a clear vista into the beyond opens out (vv. 9–11). Peter, in his first Christian sermon, felt that he must support his argument by quoting this Psalm as a forecast of the Resurrection (Acts 2: 24–28).

Psalm 17 goes a step further. Life here has not been so happy for this man as for the author of 16. He prays for the vindication of his cause, the defeat of his enemies and for the abiding sense of God's protection (vv. 5–14). In the last verse, "as for me, I shall behold thy face in righteousness; when I awake, I shall be satisfied with beholding thy form", this Psalm which contains no reference to Sheol seems to be reaching out to the thought of a far-off reward. If the quality of our life here is right, the knowledge and fellowship of God we at present enjoy will ensure the eternal vision of God's face, when the sleep of death is ended.

In such Psalms we approach the teaching of our Lord. The only argument for immortality which Jesus ever advanced was in the words "I am the God of Abraham, and the God of Isaac, and the God of Jacob. He is not God of the dead, but of the living" (Matthew 22 : 32). These words mean that, because God graciously entered into a personal relationship with these men in their lifetime, they are alive still, for such a relationship cannot be broken by death. Also, when he said to His disciples, "Because I live, you will live also" (John 14 : 19), He was stating the same argument, for He was speaking to men who had achieved personal communion with Him by surrender and faith—a relationship which cannot be severed by accident, disease or old age. Out of the very heart of that relationship Paul is able to trumpet forth the assurance: "I am sure that neither death, nor life, nor angels, nor principalities, nor things present, nor things to come, nor powers, nor height, nor depth, nor anything else in all creation, will be able to separate us from the love of God in Christ Jesus our Lord" (Romans 8 : 38–39).

4

THE POWER OF THE PSALTER

To ASK the question "Is the message of the Psalms meaning-
ful for the twentieth century?" is to raise that same issue for the
Old Testament as a whole, in its vital, powerful unity with the
New Testament. For every significant religious idea of any part
of the Old Testament re-echoes in the Psalms. Worshippers in
any century who employ the Psalms as a medium of worship are
confronted with these ideas, even as they are confronted with the
facts of their own time. Is there a connection between the ideas
enshrined in what people sing or chant and the facts which press
in so hard upon them in the modern period and which sometimes
appear to have such ominous possibilities for the future?

The Psalter's Fundamentals

In several ways the world out of which the Psalms come is a
world far off from ours. The changes have been vast, and the
speed of change is fast. In outlook and attitude, in grasp of religious conviction and scale of events, the contemporary scene is
immeasurably removed from the Biblical setting. In its funda-
mentals, however, human nature and need have not changed.
The kind of world in which we live, with all its rapid expansion
of scientific knowledge and application, has not altered and can

never alter the very constitution of human beings. The emotions of the soul are the same, and God is the same.

What has been said in previous chapters on these emotions and on His glory in Nature, History and Judgment is completely up-to-date. Especially is this so for those who, in such a world as ours, seek a faith that works amid the puzzles and trials of life, though often it has to be a faith that asks many questions, but continues strong when some of them remain unanswered. At every conspicuous point of the Psalms that faith is to be met.

In the Psalms we are called back to the deep view of life. Life in modern times has become progressively shallower. It was almost inevitable, with the quick pace of everything, the rush of life, the many things to do and hear and see. For a world which needs above all else to recover the dimension of depth, the Psalms have much to say. If we are "to live from a great depth of being", we have to turn to Him who "gave them drink as out of great depths". The perils of shallow living are serious—with shallow views of what life is for, what God is like, what sin is. It is not given to man to scale the heights without first of all going down to the depths. What Paul describes as the depths or deep things of God (1 Corinthians 2: 10) can be very unacceptable and unpalatable to earthly-minded people. In the Psalms, as in the Bible generally, the adjective "deep" is not restricted to the dark and fearful side of life, misery, doubt, despair; but is used frequently for joy, insight, penitence, purpose and victorious experience. The poorest, meanest experiences of life are the shallow ones, and the richest are the profound ones. If living on the surface is the outstanding mark of the world's life in general and to some extent of the Church's life also, there is urgent need to recapture the emphasis of the Psalms. Worship, prayer, study of the Bible, and action would all be nourished thereby.

It is indeed hard to state briefly what is the dominant theme of the Psalms. But we come near it when we say that there are two emphases in the Psalms, closely intertwined and not to be artificially separated—the personal nearness of the Most High God to nations and to individuals, and the availability of God to men for all needs and in all circumstances. All this is possible because God "reaches down to raise me" (Psalm 18: 16, Moffatt). To be sure, these are thoughts which are falteringly held and lacking in full reality until the Messiah appears. But these thoughts which may be difficult to discern in the books of the Law and even in the prophets, vibrate forcefully in the Psalms. The idea of the love of God was familiar as early as King David's time (61: 1–5; 103: 13). All the passages which speak of God's compassion bear on this—86: 15; 103: 8, 11; 145: 8–9; 63: 3; and repeatedly in 136. The personal nearness of God in the full Christian sense is not to be expected in the Psalms, for in the New Testament "Father" is the completest of all God's titles. But it is clearly foreshadowed not only in the passages from the Psalms just noted, but in Exodus 4: 22; Deuteronomy 14: 1; 32: 6; Isaiah 1: 2; 63: 16; 64: 8; Jeremiah 31: 9; Hosea 11: 1; Malachi 2: 10; 3: 17. The Old Testament contribution is that it is the Creator, King and Judge of all who is our Father. God is transcendent, but not aloof, powerful but not capricious—"the Father of an infinite Majesty".

Can we now dare to select a few Psalms which best set forth the dominant message of the whole collection? Such a selection is bound to be somewhat personal and almost biased, but no error will be fallen into if four of the best-known and most widely-read of the Psalms are chosen for this final summary—23, 46, 121 and 139.

Psalm 23 breathes the spirit of serene confidence in every verse, but this is not attained without spiritual conflict, as the references to "the valley of the shadow of death" and "in the presence of my enemies" show. Although the association of this Psalm with Jacob at Bethel (Genesis 28) is a tradition for which it is hard to find a firm foundation, the dominant thought of the Psalm— God's personal protection—has meaning enough for Jacob's situation there. The relationship between the shepherd and his sheep, so emphasized by Jesus Christ as standing for His own Person and function (John 10), is something close and special. There is a God who exercises a special care over us at all times, even when the shadows gather dark.

For many people the first passage of the Bible they ever learned by heart is Psalm 23. We can be sure that Jesus too learned it from Mary at Nazareth. It covers the whole span of life from childhood to old age and death. Some of the descriptions given to it are memorable—"the most complete picture of happiness that has ever been drawn", "the nightingale among the Psalms", "a harp with six strings"; and everyone who has ever loved it would agree that it was a blessed day when it was born. In its opening words it assures us that we belong to God as persons. Sheep do not usually see very far, but they are very good at knowing voices. The God who knows us one by one is wholly necessary to us, and we are not taking liberties when we believe that. All our needs are met in Him and by Him, and so we do not want. Even as things are in the world, people are provided for; and, where there is want, sometimes on a large scale, it is because God's liberal provision is being disturbed or wasted by man's selfishness, ignorance, or greed.

Every life needs its resting-places, and we reach them in verse 2.

The pastures are green, and green is a most restful colour. To be led by one who is deeply concerned for us is a happy experience, and especially when we know that we are to be led to still waters. In the country where the Psalms took origin, there were often days of scorching sunshine, making travel hard, and leaving people weary and exhausted; but the good shepherd knows the kind of place where he can bring his flock for shelter and pasture. These are two constant needs of the sheep, and for God's human flock it is just the same. Sheep will never rest so long as they are exposed too much to the fierce glare of the sun, and sheep are never known to lie down when they are hungry. God is with His people in the changing conditions of life, and we are asked to trust in His power to provide us with rest and food.

The scene is changed in verse 3. The quiet places are now left behind, and the shepherd and his sheep are out on the move again. For some sheep this may soon prove more than they are able to bear, and the good shepherd knows how to revive and restore them. In the life of the soul there are "fainting fits"—the lamp of faith burns low and there is even the fear that it might soon go out. Uncertainties increase, the sense of purpose and destiny grows feeble; and some way has to be found to turn back to God for reviving. Personal misfortune, the slow advance of goodness in this world, over-absorption in the material things, our own neglect of prayer and worship—all these are causes of soul-sickness. The shepherd seeks to bring back the wandering sheep and to keep them to the right tracks.

Psalm 23 goes on to give a faithful, honest picture of real life, when in verse 4 it introduces the shadows of darkness and death. Some have criticized this psalm for being inartistic, by thrusting forward these aspects of life amid all the beauty and confidence of the other verses; but it is utterly true to life. Nor is it just the experience of death that is being spoken of in it. That is certainly

included, but there are many other "glens of gloom" (Moffatt)
—disappointment, failure, remorse, bitterness, temptation. For
these occasions, as for the darkest valley of all, God has His ways
of leading us. It is not said that we shall not meet evil, but that we
shall not fear it. To be sure of the Shepherd is no guarantee of
escape from trouble and toil, but of being upheld in them. The
rod was a heavy, strong club to keep off the attacker, the staff was
a long pole with a crook with which sheep are held back or rescued from a ravine. A wise old man said that he noticed that
people most need a staff when they are going downhill.

The metaphor of the shepherd and the sheep is now left
behind, and in its place we have the picture of the host receiving
guests at a well-spread table. At the feast of life God presides.
The traveller comes at the end of the day, or the fugitive comes
fleeing before his enemies. The ancient custom was that the
traveller was welcomed, the fugitive protected, as they sought
sanctuary with the host. In the latter case, people were almost
driven to the host; and in many conditions people are driven
back to God, in danger, distress, helplessness. When the soul
of man comes to the feast of God, which He is able to spread even
in the wilderness (Psalm 78: 19), the great enemies of the soul
are kept at a distance—the tormented conscience, the power of
strong temptation, the deep desire to live for self only, fretfulness
about the uncertain future, and fear of death.

All that we need to know, and all that we can at present understand, is given to us in the resounding assurances of verse 6.
The tenses are future. It is a harder and a braver thing to say
"goodness and mercy shall follow me all the days of my life"
than to testify that they have followed thus far. This psalmist
sees no room for doubting that the experience of which the past
is so full will be repeated in the future, and so he faces the future
fearlessly. He has so much reason to know that God is good that

89

for days to come he has a sure, final trust. It might even be said that goodness and mercy are God's two sheep-dogs, coming up in the rear and following our steps. This is an idea akin to Francis Thompson's conception of God as "the Hound of Heaven". It takes all kinds of days to make a life, but the promise is for all the days. The closing picture is of one coming home and staying home—the great, lovely dream which comes true at the end of the road.

The Psalm of Providence

Psalm 46 is a more robust Psalm than 23, and deals with wider issues. It is written against a background of tumult and change, falling kingdoms, and the desolations of war. The writer is not thinking in terms of escape from all this when he appeals to his soul to "be still and know that I am God" (vv. 10–11). It is rather that he should take time calmly and quietly to recognize that God is at work in these shattering experiences, and that it is He who in the end will make wars cease to the ends of the earth. A strong belief in an over-ruling Providence which is able to make even the wrath of man to praise Him is a great bulwark in troubled days. A faith like that speaks right home to the conditions of the modern age. It is those who have learned how to possess their souls in quiet who are most confident and strong in hard times. Verse 4 seems to suggest that the way to nurture such serenity of soul is in worship. Those who neglect or despise that can have no sanctuary or citadel at all. "There is a river whose streams make glad the city of God, the holy habitation of the Most High. God is in the midst of her, she shall not be moved; God will help her right early."

This is the kind of psalm which provides the best answer to the charge that religion is really a delusion. This itself is a very ancient delusion, and some great minds have been and still are victims of it. The three most common criticisms of religion are that it does harm by introducing us to the bondage of a world of phantasy, that it does not work by supplying strength and comfort which the irreligious can equally find in their own way, and that it turns out on close examination to be wishful thinking. All this is modern enough. But the religion of Psalm 46 does not hold out any promise that it will make life merely comfortable. It does say that, when the attack is on, faith will provide new courage and power, the necessary equipment for resolute and honourable life. It seems one of the most obvious facts of history that the people who have made most of life and contributed most to life are precisely those who reach the relationship with God which the writer of Psalm 46 occupies—"God is our refuge and strength, a very present help in trouble; therefore we will not fear though the earth should change."

The Psalm of the Keeper

Life for the most part is spent in the valleys. where men live and work. So it is of great importance to meet God in the valleys down amid ordinary life and work; and He is a God of the valleys as well as of the hills (1 Kings 20: 28). The writer of Psalm 121 is in reflective mood, carrying on a meditation with himself. At the centre of his thoughts is Jerusalem, set on a hill, surrounded by hills. He puts to himself the question "From whence does my help come?" and he replies that "my help comes from the Lord, who made heaven and earth". In his mind also there is the thought which has always been strong in the human mind that the divine power or powers dwelt among the mountains—"as the mountains are round about Jerusalem, so the Lord is round about his people" (125: 2).

From the mountains we learn great thoughts of God (115: 15; 124: 8; 134: 3; 146: 6). There is no religious need of the modern world greater than the recovery of the sense of the supremacy and majesty of God which has almost passed away from many minds. God is and forever must remain a tremendous mystery, awe-inspiring at all times, before which all that we can do is to bow in wondering silence. The mysteriousness of great mountains is a fit symbol of God. In a rapidly-changing world they speak also of what is unchangeable from age to age. There is a perpetual steadfastness in the hills pointing us to a God who is completely faithful, on whom men can absolutely depend.

The psalmist proceeds to strengthen his faith by recalling that this great God is the Keeper of Israel (Deuteronomy 32: 9) and his own Keeper too. If the high mountains might have conveyed to him the impression of his own insignificance before them and before God, this is all corrected and removed by the convictions of personal care and kindness which are the Psalm's main theme. God is as near to us as He can be, at our right hand (v. 5), and so we are protected day and night by a God of unsleeping watchfulness (vv. 3–7). This psalm has sometimes been described as offering "a blessing for the threshold"—"the Lord will keep your going out and your coming in from this time forth and for evermore" (v. 8; cf. Deuteronomy 28: 6; 31: 2). Life consists in a continual going out and coming in, over the varied thresholds of home and duty. This is so for everybody. There is an inescapable routine in life; but all the difference is made by living out that routine in the company and defence of

God—we shall walk up and down in the name of the Lord (Micah 4: 5). If the teaching of Psalm 121 is really true, life is indeed very good, and it has a goodness that knows no end, "for evermore".

The Psalm of the All Wise God

Psalm 139 is the finest example of all of the idea of a God who knows us through and through (vv. 1–6), from whom it is not possible for man to hide (vv. 7–12). To believe in such a God is the source of all true reverence and confidence.

There are three main attitudes which may be taken up to facts—we can refuse to see them, we can recognize them with a grudge, we can rejoice in them. This Psalm opens with the simple statement that God searches us and knows us, it ends with the earnest prayer that this may go on continually (v. 23). In other words, the writer is taking the right attitude to the facts. He has three things to say about God. God knows everything (cf. Psalm 17: 3; Jeremiah 17: 10), our whole life in rest and activity, our thoughts, our words and all our ways; so we are hemmed in and besieged by God, and there is no escape (v. 5). God is everywhere, in earth, and heaven and hell, and there is no possibility of travelling beyond His influence. God has also fashioned and ordered our life from the beginning, in a way that is fearful and wonderful (vv. 13–18). Accordingly man can keep no secrets from God, nor ever hide himself from God by distance or by darkness; and so the writer is utterly willing that God should search him and try him and know his thoughts. It is in this way that we are kept humble before God, kept watchful about what we admit into our life, kept thankful for His patience

93

with us, and kept hopeful because He who knows all will take all He knows into His judgment of us.

The choice which this Psalm sets before us is between the futile course of hiding from God and the fertile course of submitting to be led by God in the way everlasting (v. 24). The former is as old as Adam and Eve who at the very beginning of things took what steps they could to hide from God, but they discovered that God's voice can reach us wherever we are. The "hidden man of the heart" is naked and open to the eyes of Him with whom we have to do. There are times when God seems to hide from us—Deuteronomy 31: 17–18; Isaiah 45: 15; 57: 17; Ezekiel 39: 23–24. One of the great prayers of the Psalms is "Hide not thy face from me" (27: 9). The ways in which men attempt to escape from God are many—by engrossing ourselves in a very busy life, by plunging into a very hectic life of pleasure, by excessive pride in our own powers of intellect or in the success that we seem to have made of life, by a shallow and conventional association with places and acts of worship, by a refusal to make an honest, fearless stand, and by half-hearted examination of ourselves before God. These are the great enemies of the soul. To all this Psalm 139 is a splendid corrective. For God Himself, in a grand, unique sense, is our Hiding-Place (Psalms 17: 8; 27: 5, 9; 32: 7; 119: 114). In the Christian revelation this reaches out and up to the experience of having our "life hid with Christ in God" (Colossians 3: 3).

The alternative to the way of escape is the way everlasting. This closing phrase of the Psalm is not to be interpreted as if it referred to the life to come and nothing else. Like other Psalms, this Psalm has been describing an immediate communion with God which holds at its heart the promise that death will not be able to break it off. But we begin to walk the way everlasting here and now. Whenever we set our feet to avenues which lead

94

to fuller and ever fuller life, we are upon the way everlasting. This psalmist is not able to get out of his mind the fact that there are men who "maliciously defy thee, who lift themselves up against thee for evil" (v. 20). They are the enemies of God, and for that reason his enemies too, and so he "hates them with perfect hatred". But it would be very dangerous to say that kind of thing about others without at the same time confessing that the same kind of condition might well enter our own life, and we have no reason to be over-sure of ourselves—and so at once the prayer follows: "Search me and know me and try me." Only then does the way everlasting open.

The marks of those who are walking this way are simple trust amid changing circumstances, a disinterested ambition to make the most of life, a continual willingness to learn and to be led further and further into the knowledge of God, a discipline of life under the rule of God, and a tireless spirit of service and helpfulness to others. If the nearness of God of which this Psalm is so full is a fact in man's experience, these are the ways in which it will be evident. And there is no need to fear that the way everlasting may come to a dead stop. The guarantee against that is the assertion about God with which Psalm 100 closes, quoted from the metrical version:

> For why, the Lord our God is good,
> His mercy is for ever sure;
> His truth at all times firmly stood,
> And shall from age to age endure.